Table of Contents

Chapter 1: Doubt in the Mirror

John stared at his reflection in the bathroom mirror, studying his face as if he could find in its lines and angles some answer, some buried truth he'd overlooked. He leaned in closer, scrutinizing the faint creases at the corners of his eyes, the slight tension in his brow, looking for some sign he might have missed—a clue, maybe, that would make him feel *present* in his own life. For years, he had inhabited this face, this body, this image of himself, and yet, standing here, he felt like a stranger. It was a strange, unsettling feeling, as though he were observing someone else, a man who looked and sounded like him but lived a life that felt increasingly foreign.

He was a man on the rise, or so everyone said. His boss praised him openly; his colleagues threw admiring glances his way. John had become the "go-to guy," the model of what a sales executive should be—reliable, persuasive, polished. There was no shortage of affirmations: *"John's got the charm,"* they'd say, or *"He could sell ice to an Eskimo."* He'd heard these things about himself so often that he could practically recite them in his sleep. Yet, in moments like this, alone with his reflection, the words felt hollow, like phrases from a script he'd been reciting his whole life without understanding their meaning.

He leaned even closer, his breath misting the glass as he examined his face from inches away. His jaw was set in that confident, square line he'd learned to adopt, a look that exuded authority. Sharp, reliable—qualities he'd always thought of as strengths. His chin bore the faintest trace of stubble, a shadow that had just started to come through. He ran his hand over it, feeling the roughness, feeling *something*, and for a fleeting moment, he wondered if that was all he was—a collection of carefully crafted traits and expressions he'd pieced together to meet the expectations of others.

Above him, the light buzzed softly, casting sharp shadows over his face, exaggerating the angles, making him look sharper, harder. It felt like a spotlight, a stage light, illuminating him in this private moment where he was laid bare, stripped of pretense. He let his gaze drift downward to the suit hanging on the back of the door—classic gray, expertly tailored, the kind of suit that commanded respect without demanding it. It was his armor, his uniform. The suit itself was yet another projection of John: crisp, confident, unassuming in a way that made him easy to trust. In it, he was John the Closer, the Salesman, the Man of Numbers, someone who could walk into a room and make people listen. But now, looking at that suit, he felt an odd disconnect. It was a shell, something he slipped into each morning, as though it were his entire identity.

Is that who I am? The question lingered in the air, unspoken but heavy, as he looked back at his reflection. In the mirror, he tried to see himself as others saw him—

the friendly but assertive sales executive, the charming negotiator, the man who made things happen. But as he looked deeper, he felt a strange sense of emptiness creeping in, a void that felt unfillable no matter how many sales he closed or quotas he hit. It was as though he'd spent so long constructing this version of himself that he'd forgotten what lay beneath, if there was anything beneath at all.

He remembered the compliments, the congratulations, the pats on the back from his boss. He'd hit target after target, received award after award. His LinkedIn profile gleamed with endorsements, his professional image meticulously crafted. But the strange truth was that none of it felt real. They were just words, just images, just expectations he had fulfilled so diligently, so automatically, that they felt as though they belonged to someone else. And maybe they did. Maybe "John" was just a role he'd been playing for so long that he'd lost sight of who he actually was.

He closed his eyes, feeling the weight of it, the exhaustion that came from sustaining a facade. There was a part of him that wanted to pull away from this reflection, to stop thinking, to push aside these thoughts that threatened the structure he'd built so carefully. But something kept him there, rooted to the spot, forcing him to look deeper. And as he looked, he couldn't ignore the hollowness that stared back at him—a man with everything going for him on paper but an ache inside, an ache for something different, something real.

What did "real" even mean? The thought struck him suddenly, catching him off guard. He had built a life that ticked all the boxes, that matched every expectation society, his family, and even he had set for himself. But why did it feel so thin, so insubstantial? He felt like a shadow of himself, a well-dressed silhouette going through the motions, ticking off achievements like items on a checklist, never stopping to question why. *Who am I doing this for?* he thought, a quiet desperation edging into the question.

He glanced back at the suit hanging on the door, suddenly seeing it differently, as though it were a costume he was tired of wearing. Day after day, he put it on, buttoned it up, and transformed himself into John, the man everyone expected him to be. But beneath the suit, he was just... *him*. The man staring back in the mirror didn't feel quite like John, didn't feel like the sales executive, the "closer." He was someone else—someone who had dreams, doubts, insecurities, someone who wanted more than just the next sale or the next promotion.

Lately, John had been caught in a loop of strange, wandering thoughts. They came in waves, interrupting the automatic rhythm of his daily routine. Sometimes it was a passing question that lingered far longer than he expected, whispering to him like an insistent breeze he couldn't shake. Today, the question was particularly vivid. *What would it be like,* he wondered, *if I weren't the person staring back at me in this mirror? What if... what if I were someone else? Someone... different? A woman?*

He hadn't shared this line of thinking with anyone, not even his closest friends. It was too strange, too abstract—something he was only half-sure he even understood himself.

The initial thought had struck him during a meeting. It was a mundane Monday morning review, a room full of salespeople around the polished conference table. The client they were discussing was notoriously difficult, particularly toward male reps. As the head of the department laid out strategy after strategy, John's mind had wandered, wondering whether his female colleagues faced these challenges in quite the same way. There were certain clients, after all, who warmed up instantly to women, yet stayed cool and guarded with men. He'd seen it time and time again, in subtle ways: the warm smile a male client gave to a female colleague, the moments they were heard more easily, even indulged a bit, where he was scrutinized.

Sitting in that meeting, he found himself caught up in an odd curiosity, his mind racing with possibilities. Would they talk to him differently? Trust him in ways they didn't now? And beyond his career, how would he be treated in day-to-day life? He'd never seriously considered these questions before, but now, once the door cracked open, he couldn't stop himself from pushing it further. It was strange how this curiosity—this *doubt*—seemed to take on a life of its own, simmering beneath the surface of his thoughts, pulling him back to it when he least expected.

After that meeting, it was as if he saw himself in a double exposure: half the man he'd always been, and half someone else he didn't yet understand. Every glance in the mirror seemed to carry with it this nagging question. He began to imagine what life would look like if he weren't bound by his current self. What if he could approach life from a different angle, step into a new perspective?

John didn't dislike being a man, or even his life, but there were times he felt confined by expectations that came with it. The subtle but insistent pressure to assert, to be competent, to constantly perform with little room for vulnerability. He wondered if women felt this same weight, or if their burden was a different shape entirely. In the world of sales, these expectations were magnified; success demanded confidence and charm, yet both felt increasingly performative to him. Was he really connecting with people? Or was he simply delivering the version of himself that clients expected to see?

These thoughts haunted him most at night, when he was alone with them. He'd lie in bed, staring at the ceiling, and try to push them aside, only for them to creep back, persistent and unyielding. Was it so strange, he wondered, to want to step into another's life? To know what it would feel like, not just to "see" the world through someone else's eyes but to live it? It was a thought that made him feel oddly alive, yet there was an uneasiness to it, a discomfort in realizing that he wasn't entirely satisfied with who he'd become.

One morning, while preparing for another day at work, John found himself staring into the mirror once more. But today was different. Today, he wasn't just pondering abstract possibilities—he was staring straight at his reflection, searching for something. *What if I wasn't looking at John?* he thought, almost on instinct. *What if I were looking at someone else?*

The idea took root, spreading quickly. He watched his face, but in his mind, it began to shift, to soften. A slight narrowing at the jaw, a gentler arch to the brows. He could almost see it—another person emerging behind the mask he had always worn, a person who lived somewhere within him yet felt so far away. She seemed to wait there, quietly, in his reflection, as if she'd always been a part of him, and he had simply never taken the time to notice her.

"Jane," he murmured, the sound barely escaping his lips, a whisper so faint it felt as though it had come from somewhere else. The name echoed softly in his mind, unexpected yet strangely familiar, like a tune he'd once known by heart but had long since forgotten. He was surprised at how natural it sounded, how easily it rolled off his tongue, and yet the way it hung in the air felt transformative, almost sacred. *Jane.* As he repeated it to himself, he felt a spark of something—a quiet thrill, like the beginning of an adventure he had never dared to imagine.

John felt his heart beat faster. He took in his reflection with new eyes, studying the contours and shadows of his face, searching for more traces of her, as though Jane had always been there, hiding in the depths of his gaze. There was a beauty in this feeling, an almost giddy sensation that washed over him, like a rush of adrenaline. A sense of anticipation bubbled up in his chest, a feeling he hadn't experienced in years—perhaps not since he was a boy dreaming of all the lives he could live, all the people he could be. It was as if he were standing on the edge of something vast and unknown, yet deeply intimate, waiting to step into a world that was his yet wasn't. The thought was exhilarating.

But beneath the thrill, a thread of doubt wove its way into his mind. *What am I doing?* The question broke through like a discordant note, jarring him from his reverie. The familiar voice of reason that had guided him throughout his life spoke up, cautioning him, reminding him of all the ways in which this was impractical, strange, maybe even absurd. *You're John,* he thought firmly, as if saying it to himself would tether him back to reality. John. The steady, reliable sales executive. The man who knew how to close a deal and charm a room, who had the respect of his colleagues, who wore the same brand of cologne and tailored suits, day in and day out.

But then, why did "Jane" feel so *right*? Why did that name, that person, feel so comfortable, almost inevitable, as though she had been there all along, waiting for him to finally notice her? The thought unsettled him and thrilled him all at once. He felt like an explorer venturing into uncharted territory, both drawn to and terrified by what he might find.

He found himself wanting to try on her skin, to see the world through her eyes, to understand who *she* was. Who *he* was, really, underneath all the layers that had been imposed on him—the expectations, the routine, the well-worn path he'd walked since he was old enough to know what was expected of him. There was a strange sense of freedom in this possibility, an invitation to live differently, to step outside of himself, to shed the constraints of "John" and discover someone new.

A vision of Jane came to life in his mind. She was still him, yet not him—a woman with a softness and vulnerability he rarely showed, yet with a quiet strength that seemed to rise from somewhere deeper, somewhere true. He imagined her in conversation, her words flowing with a subtle warmth that put others at ease, a kindness in her voice that people found inviting. She was composed yet approachable, driven but with a gentleness that softened her edges. Where John's confidence was honed from years of practice and self-discipline, Jane's felt effortless, as though she knew who she was in a way John had never allowed himself to.

But with each new vision of Jane, he also felt the uncertainty grow, blooming darkly within him. *What if this isn't real? What if it's just a fantasy?* The questions circled like dark clouds, warning him of the risks, of the judgments he might face, of the rejection and confusion that would certainly arise if he allowed himself to explore this new identity. He thought of his colleagues, his family, his friends. What would they say? Would they see him as unhinged, someone having a midlife crisis or worse? The thought made his heart pound with fear, but it didn't quell the desire to explore this new side of himself, to find out who Jane really was.

The mirror reflected the flicker of conflict in his eyes, a tension he didn't know how to resolve. Part of him wanted to turn away, to shut this down, to get back to his routine and let "Jane" fade into the recesses of his mind, a fleeting curiosity never to be revisited. But he couldn't. Not now. The thrill of discovery was too enticing, and for the first time in a long time, he felt truly alive.

There was a surprising softness to the name "Jane," a kind of simplicity that called to him, inviting him into a life that was less performative, less weighed down by the expectations he felt as John. As Jane, he could be gentle, introspective, present. There would be no need to project an air of authority or constantly prove himself. It was as though Jane allowed him to drop his armor, to be vulnerable, unguarded. The idea of stepping into her life felt liberating, a chance to escape the rigid boundaries he had set for himself.

John lingered there, savoring the sensation. *What if?* The question pulsed in his mind, urging him forward, tempting him to continue down this path, to explore this unknown territory within himself. He took a deep breath, allowing himself to embrace the fantasy, to imagine what it would be like if he allowed Jane to live—not as a thought, but as a reality.

Chapter 2: Seeds of Curiosity

It started as a quiet thought, something vague that he could ignore if he wanted to. It was a small curiosity—tiny, but potent, like a single drop of ink spreading through water. John had always been the steady, consistent figure in his office, the man with the sharp suit, the reliable sales pitch, the one who always knew how to read a room. But lately, the way he was reading people, particularly his female colleagues, had started to shift in a way he didn't expect.

It began in the conference room, during a strategy meeting that was routine in every way except for what he began to notice. They were discussing a difficult client, Mr. Crosswell, a high-profile CEO with a reputation for being demanding, especially with sales reps. Everyone around the table tossed around strategies, talking over each other in that corporate way that made John feel like they were all competing for attention. But his mind kept drifting back to the last few calls he'd been on with Crosswell. He'd often felt he had to adjust his tone, assert himself more to make his ideas heard, almost bending over backward to project confidence. Yet the moment Rachel, a quiet but perceptive member of his team, suggested a softer approach, one that might make Crosswell feel more at ease, John noticed a shift in the room's energy.

Rachel's idea was smart, clever even—it suggested she understood their client better than the rest. But as she spoke, John saw the subtle cues from around the table: a few faint smirks, raised eyebrows, the quick glance

Martin, the team leader, exchanged with their boss. Martin's response was cordial but dismissive, something about "keeping a firm stance with high-stakes clients." John didn't think much of it at first, but he couldn't shake the feeling that Rachel's suggestion had been shot down prematurely, not for lack of merit but for reasons he couldn't quite pinpoint.

As the meeting wore on, John's gaze drifted to Rachel, sitting there composed, her hands folded over her notes, her lips pressed together in a polite, neutral line. It was as though she were wearing a mask, a thin veil of patience hiding something deeper, something vulnerable and unspoken. He knew she was disappointed; he saw it in the way her fingers gripped the edge of her notebook, her eyes focused down on the page as if it were a shield. He felt an odd pang of frustration on her behalf. Had it been him suggesting that approach, he knew it would've been considered. The others would have at least discussed it, if not adopted it.

For the rest of the day, John carried that sense of unease with him. He caught himself watching Rachel and his other female colleagues with fresh eyes, almost as if he were seeing them for the first time. Michelle from marketing, a woman with sharp instincts and a genuine warmth, always tempered her voice when speaking to higher-ups, choosing words carefully, opting for phrases like, "If I may suggest..." or "Just a thought..." John thought back to his own meetings with management. He'd never felt the need to preface his ideas, to pad his words with safety nets and apologies. He wondered if

Michelle even noticed she was doing it, or if it was so ingrained in her that she'd stopped thinking about it years ago.

As the days passed, John's curiosity evolved from a fleeting thought into something that felt like a slow, smoldering fire, compelling him to pay closer attention to the world around him. It was like peeling back a layer he hadn't even known was there. He found himself observing his female colleagues, his eyes lingering on details he would've missed before, tiny moments that seemed loaded with meaning. At first, he brushed off his own thoughts as overthinking, an odd fascination that would surely pass. But the more he watched, the more he began to see things that shook him, things he couldn't ignore.

One afternoon, he was grabbing a quick lunch in the break room when he overheard Maya, one of the junior executives, talking animatedly to a small group about her latest client meeting. Maya was sharp and determined, a fast-rising star with an easy laugh that made people gravitate toward her. As she recounted her story, she was laughing, but it was a humor laced with something bitter. She told the group about her frustrating meeting with a new client, who had called her "sweetheart" no fewer than three times, his voice laced with a patronizing charm that bordered on condescension. She mimicked his voice with a slight roll of her eyes, a forced smile on her face. "He just kept calling me 'sweetheart,'" she said, "as if that's supposed to make me feel... what? Small? Less than?"

The room laughed with her, but it was the kind of laughter that felt uneasy, almost defensive. John watched her closely, sensing that beneath her story was a quiet frustration that her laughter couldn't hide. There was a tightness in her smile, a flicker in her eyes as she pushed the discomfort away, brushing it off as if it were just another part of the job, as if this was something she was used to, something that came with the territory. The group laughed along, exchanging sympathetic glances, but John felt something deeper—a gnawing sense of unfairness. It unsettled him, this casual way Maya shrugged off behavior that felt so out of place, so belittling. She told her story as if it were a joke, as if the only way she could truly process the experience was by stripping it of its weight. But John could see, in the way she shifted her posture and forced herself to chuckle, that she didn't find it funny at all.

As he watched her, John felt a surprising anger simmering beneath his surface. He realized that he'd never had to deal with anything quite like that. Clients respected him, valued his ideas, and took his presence seriously. They might tease or joke with him in passing, but he'd never felt his professional identity reduced to something as trivial as a pet name. He'd always felt like he had a rightful place at the table, an unspoken authority that was simply granted. *Would anyone ever think to call him 'sweetheart'?* The very idea felt ridiculous, and the absurdity of it made him feel suddenly complicit, as though he'd been benefiting from a privilege he'd never even known he had.

It wasn't just the clients, though. The more he listened, the more he noticed stories his female colleagues shared that hinted at a double standard that existed within the company itself, woven into the very fabric of their day-to-day. One afternoon, he overheard Rachel, one of the top sales performers, talking about some feedback she'd received during her last performance review. Rachel was sharp, no-nonsense, with a work ethic that left others struggling to keep up. Yet John heard her mention, almost offhandedly, how her manager had encouraged her to be "more approachable" in her client meetings, to "soften" her tone and "be herself" more.

John had been in the same reviews, and he couldn't recall anyone ever giving him advice on his tone, his posture, or his mannerisms. The idea of someone telling him to "smile more" was almost laughable. If anything, he knew that his quiet, sometimes serious demeanor had only ever served to enhance his reputation. His colleagues respected his focus, his ability to stay calm under pressure. And yet, here was Rachel, with numbers and performance that spoke for themselves, being told to adjust her personality, to dial herself back. She was one of the most successful people in the room, yet somehow that wasn't enough.

The realization unsettled him, this invisible force that seemed to dictate how his colleagues were expected to act simply because they were women. He couldn't shake the feeling that, had it been him, the advice would have been different—more practical, less personal, and, above all, less condescending. He started to wonder just how often Rachel heard this kind of feedback. Was it a one-off comment, or was it part of the background noise she had to deal with every day?

The thought stayed with him, festering into something uncomfortable and raw. He remembered Rachel's face as she recounted the feedback, her expression caught between forced neutrality and a simmering resentment that she'd kept carefully controlled. He imagined what it would feel like to be constantly told to smile, to appear friendly, to soften every edge of himself just to make others feel more at ease. Would he feel like he was always on a stage, his real self obscured behind a performance that he hadn't chosen?

The more he thought about it, the angrier he felt—not just for Rachel, but for himself, for all the times he'd unknowingly benefited from this unspoken advantage. He hadn't noticed it before because he hadn't *had* to. The rules for him were different; he'd played the game with a set of advantages he hadn't even known he'd been given. And with each passing day, that realization weighed on him more heavily, turning from a vague curiosity into a pressing need to understand.

It was as if he were standing at the edge of a cliff, looking down into something vast and unknown. He could sense that there was a world he'd never seen, one that was hidden behind the familiarity of his day-to-day life. And he wanted to know it, to feel what his colleagues felt, to experience the invisible weight they carried with them every day.

One afternoon, John found himself walking through the office, noticing the small, nearly invisible details around him with fresh eyes. A male colleague gave a presentation to the team, using confident, assertive language that made his pitch sound bulletproof, even though the proposal was half-formed. Then Michelle presented her idea, careful and well-prepared, her voice measured, her delivery polished. Yet the room responded to her differently, with a cool, cautious approval that lacked the easy enthusiasm John was used to receiving.

He felt the disconnect deeply, the sense that the room held his male colleagues to a different standard, one that felt easier, less scrutinized. It was subtle, unspoken, a bias that floated through the room like smoke. John could feel it settling around him, making him realize just how rarely he'd ever had to question his place, his worth, his ability to be heard. He wondered what it would be like to be under that kind of microscope, day in and day out.

He began to imagine how things might feel if he were in Rachel's shoes, if he'd walked through the same meetings, faced the same invisible expectations, the little words or glances that seemed to shift the atmosphere around her. The idea simmered in his mind, a nagging thought that wouldn't leave him alone. What would it be like to enter those meetings, make those calls, pitch those ideas, but from an entirely different vantage point?

The thought became a fascination, a slow-growing urge to see the world through a different lens. At night, he'd lie in bed, staring at the ceiling, replaying moments from his day, wondering what they might have felt like if he were Rachel, or Maya, or Michelle. He wondered if he'd be able to muster the same patience, the same resilience, if he knew each day that his voice might be met with skepticism, if he knew that his ideas, even the best ones, might not be heard.

As these thoughts crept into his mind, a feeling of excitement began to mingle with his curiosity—a feeling he hadn't experienced in years. It was as if he were on the edge of an adventure, a mystery to be unraveled. He began to fantasize about stepping into a life different from his own, to truly experience what it would mean to live on the other side of these unspoken rules and assumptions.

The line between curiosity and desire blurred as he realized that he didn't just *want* to understand his female colleagues' experiences—he needed to. It felt urgent, almost as if a part of himself had been waiting for this realization all along, as though this question of identity, of perspective, had always been there, lingering just beneath the surface.

Chapter 3: Imagining Jane

In the stillness of the early morning, John found himself transfixed by his reflection, as if seeing it for the first time. He leaned forward, searching the face staring back at him. He knew every line and angle, the squared jaw, the subtle furrow of his brow, the slight crease at the corner of his mouth. And yet, he felt like he was peering through a fog, catching only glimpses of someone else hiding beneath this familiar mask. This wasn't just a thought experiment anymore. Something deeper was stirring within him, a curiosity that had become an ache, an undeniable pull to explore a different version of himself.

A woman's version of himself. *Jane.* The name had appeared as if by magic, a gentle yet solid name, carrying with it the weight of someone he wanted to know intimately. *Jane.* It was a name that felt soft on his tongue but strong in his mind. Every time he thought of her, she seemed to grow more real, more vivid, until he could practically feel her presence beside him, like a shadow made of warmth and light. He was no longer simply imagining her—he was creating her, shaping her from the depths of his own being.

As he thought of her, an exhilarating question filled his mind: *What would it feel like to let Jane live?*

John couldn't hold back the excitement rising within him. He wanted to see her, feel her, to stand face to face with Jane as if she were a real person, not just a figment of his imagination. And he wanted to let her out into the world, if only for a moment. Without thinking, he let himself slip into her mind. He stood up a little straighter, softening the stern set of his jaw, relaxing the tension he always carried in his shoulders. He let his arms fall naturally to his sides, rather than in the rigid stance he usually adopted. It felt strangely freeing, as if he were shedding layers he'd carried for far too long.

What would Jane look like? The question lingered, tantalizing, as John leaned forward, closing his eyes to let the image come alive in his mind. He drew in a slow, deep breath, feeling his chest rise and fall, as if each inhale brought her closer to the surface, her presence expanding, shaping itself within him.

Jane's face began to take form, almost intuitively, as if she were someone he had always known but only just remembered. She had his same cheekbones but softened, as though carved by a gentle hand. Her brows were relaxed, carrying none of the tension that his often held after years of navigating intense meetings and high-stakes negotiations. Her face was open, welcoming, and there was something unguarded in the curve of her mouth. He imagined her lips gently parted in a way his never were—a hint of a smile, subtle yet inviting, as if she held a world of secrets and understanding behind that delicate expression.

There was warmth in her eyes, a deep, radiant warmth that he found himself drawn to, even in his imagination. Her eyes held kindness—not the restrained politeness he so often displayed in business settings, but an honest compassion, an openness that invited others in. John imagined that people would feel safe around Jane, that they would trust her without question, sensing that she truly listened, that she understood. This was a kindness he knew he carried somewhere inside himself but rarely allowed to show; it was too vulnerable, too exposed for the world he inhabited as John. But for Jane, it felt like second nature.

Her hair flowed softly around her face, framing her features with an effortless grace. In his mind, John could see it cascading gently past her shoulders, catching the light, moving with her. It softened her, added a depth and dimension to her that he found mesmerizing. She was, he realized, both strong and soft in equal measure, an embodiment of quiet power that needed no fanfare or force. She was confident, not because she fought for her place but because her place felt earned, as if she belonged simply by existing.

John's heartbeat quickened as he held her image in his mind. He could feel her presence in the room with him, subtle yet undeniable, filling the empty spaces of his own consciousness. She was becoming real, taking shape beyond just his imagination, as if she had been there all along, waiting for him to notice her. A tingling thrill washed over him, the sensation of standing on the edge of something vast, something he couldn't fully understand yet, but which beckoned him with open arms.

Opening his eyes, he felt a strange sense of calm wash over him. It was as if he were looking at himself for the first time, seeing beyond the hard lines of his jaw, the stern set of his brow, the weight he carried in his shoulders. He held Jane's image in his mind, as if anchoring her to this moment, feeling her quiet strength and poise, her gentle confidence radiate from within him. He could almost feel her standing beside him, her eyes meeting his in the mirror, her expression warm yet knowing, as if she were already aware of every doubt, every question that raced through his mind.

You're almost there, she seemed to say, her voice gentle yet certain, resonating in his mind. Let me out.

A shiver ran through him as he heard her, as if the words had come not from his imagination but from somewhere deep within, a part of him he had long neglected. The thought was thrilling and unsettling, like opening a door he'd kept locked for years. His breath quickened as he looked at his reflection, seeing not just himself but the woman he could become, the woman who seemed to be waiting just beneath the surface, ready to take her first step into the world.

John closed his eyes again, feeling her presence strengthen, as if she were standing just behind him, her hand lightly on his shoulder. He could almost feel the weight of her hand there, grounding him, urging him forward. In his mind, he imagined her speaking to him, her words gentle yet firm: It's okay. I'm here. Let me show you. The thought filled him with a strange, buoyant courage, an unexpected confidence that surged within him.

Taking a deep breath, he allowed himself to sink into her presence, to feel the calm certainty that she carried. She was composed, unafraid, untouched by the need to prove herself. She was a woman who knew her worth, who moved through the world with a confidence that came not from her achievements but from her own inner sense of belonging. She didn't need approval; she simply existed, whole and complete in herself.

With his eyes closed, he raised his hand, feeling the softness of his own touch, imagining it as Jane's hand, as if she were reaching out to meet him halfway. He traced his jawline, feeling the contours of his face, envisioning the subtle softness she would bring. She would carry her strength differently, he thought—less as a shield, more as a steady, grounded presence. She wouldn't have the need to project power because she knew it was already there.

In his mind, he imagined her at the office, walking into a meeting with that quiet poise, her presence shifting the room not because she demanded attention but because she deserved it. People would turn to her, not because she forced them to, but because they sensed her strength, her understanding, her depth. She would look people in the eyes, unflinching, with a warmth that drew them in, made them want to share with her, to trust her.

For the first time in his life, John felt what it would be like to let his guard down completely, to approach the world not from a place of defense but of acceptance. He felt her inside him, grounding him, centering him, showing him a version of himself he had only glimpsed before.

And in that moment, he knew—Jane was more than just an experiment. She was real, as real as he was, a part of him that had been waiting patiently, waiting for him to finally see her.

His heart began to race as he took the next step. He wanted to let her take over, to see what it would feel like to truly embody Jane. In the privacy of his bathroom, John opened the cabinet above the sink, his fingers grazing over the usual collection of items—shaving cream, cologne, an electric razor. But then his hand drifted over a small tube of lip balm, something he'd never paid much attention to. He picked it up, rolling it between his fingers as he felt an almost childlike thrill surge within him. *Would Jane wear it?* He unscrewed the cap, feeling a small, nervous excitement as he raised it to his lips, just the faintest tint adding a soft color.

He looked in the mirror, and to his surprise, he felt different. There was no clear, stark transformation, but somehow, it was enough. Jane was there, looking back at him. He felt her presence more strongly than ever, filling him with a sense of freedom he hadn't experienced before. He smiled at himself, an unguarded, open smile, the kind of smile he imagined Jane would wear every day if she could.

But it wasn't enough. John's heart pounded as he realized that he didn't want Jane to stay confined to his imagination or to his own private mirror. He wanted to bring her to life, fully, not just in spirit but in form. He wanted to let her see the world, to move through it as a woman and see what that would feel like, the freedom and the vulnerabilities all wrapped up in one.

The thought thrilled him. And for the first time, he knew he wouldn't be satisfied until he tried. He needed to see her in the world, to walk in her shoes, even if just for a few hours. He went online, his fingers trembling slightly as he typed out searches he'd never imagined making. His heart raced as he browsed, picking out a wig—a dark, soft wave, a contrast to his usual neat, close-cropped hair. He imagined it framing her face, softening his features, helping her feel like the woman he wanted her to be. He added a few simple makeup items to his cart, his hands tingling with excitement. It felt exhilarating and terrifying at the same time, this idea that he could actually make Jane real.

When the package arrived a few days later, he felt an odd mix of anticipation and nerves, like a secret he was keeping even from himself. He locked the door to his bedroom, the world outside vanishing as he sat on the edge of his bed and opened the box with careful hands. Inside, nestled in tissue paper, lay the wig, a simple black dress, and a small bag of makeup. The sight of them made his pulse quicken. He could feel Jane, as if she were sitting beside him, waiting patiently. He took a deep breath, the thought racing through his mind: *It's time.*

With unsteady hands, John lifted the wig, a cascade of dark waves flowing through his fingers, light as air. He held his breath as he gently placed it over his head, feeling the soft weight settle, the cool strands brushing his cheeks and neck. The hair framed his face, instantly softening his features, and he felt an unexpected warmth radiate from within, as if each lock of hair was drawing out something buried deep inside him. He watched in the mirror as his reflection began to transform, his heart pounding like a drum in his chest. The face looking back at him was still his, yet it wasn't—it was someone new, someone he wanted to know intimately.

His fingers trembled as he picked up the small tube of lip balm, this time applying it with deliberate care, as though it were a sacred ritual. The subtle pink color touched his lips with a softness he hadn't anticipated, and he saw the faintest hint of warmth bloom across his face. Each swipe felt like it was adding a new layer to the person taking shape before him. There was no hesitation now, only a growing certainty—a sense of discovery that filled him with awe and a shivering thrill. He could feel Jane awakening, her presence becoming more defined, more *real* with every stroke.

He reached for the foundation, unscrewing the cap with fingers that felt strangely steady despite the wild fluttering in his chest. He dabbed a bit onto a brush, gently sweeping it across his skin, watching as the subtle texture blurred the lines he had always known. As the foundation smoothed his complexion, he felt a strange liberation, as though he were unearthing a side of himself that had been buried under layers of expectation and duty. Stroke by stroke, he applied it, letting the gentleness and care of each motion bring him closer to Jane.

The person in the mirror wasn't quite John anymore. He felt it with each passing second, an undeniable shift, as though he were dissolving and she were emerging, soft and graceful, yet stronger than he could have imagined. There was a tenderness in her expression, an elegance that glowed softly, filling the room with an almost electric charge. Her eyes shone with warmth, a quiet confidence that held a kindness he didn't often show, a welcome that invited, accepted, embraced.

His hands shook slightly as he took the final, most daring step. He slipped out of his usual attire and into the dress he'd picked, feeling the fabric slide against his skin in a way that was both foreign and profoundly comforting. The fabric was cool and smooth, flowing around him with a lightness that made him feel like he could float, like he could drift into this new self without a trace of resistance. He felt his body relax as he adjusted the dress, letting it settle over him naturally, as though it had been waiting for him all along. He took a slow, deep breath, letting the sensation wash over him, filling him with an unexpected calm.

When he looked up, he didn't just see Jane in the mirror—he *felt* her. There she was, standing tall, her posture relaxed but graceful, her shoulders softened. His heart skipped a beat as he realized that the reflection before him was a vision he hadn't even known he needed. She was beautiful, yes, but it was more than that. She was free. She carried a gentleness that felt like an unspoken strength, a quiet power that radiated without the need to assert itself. Her eyes held a knowing, a deep understanding of who she was and the journey she'd taken to get here.

He allowed himself to fully slip into her, adjusting his posture as if shedding his former self like an old coat. He let his shoulders relax, his neck elongate, his stance become softer yet confident. In that moment, he was no longer a man trying to imagine himself as a woman. He *was* Jane, the woman who had been waiting in the wings, the woman who had always been there, hidden just beneath the surface. She smiled—a gentle, genuine smile, not the practiced smirk he had used to charm clients, but a smile that felt like the purest version of himself.

It was like coming home to a place he had never known existed. Jane felt real, vivid, vibrant in a way that made the room seem brighter, sharper. She looked at herself with an expression of awe, her eyes glistening with the knowledge that this was more than just a transformation—it was a revelation. She lifted her hand, touching her face lightly, fingers tracing over her cheek as if reassuring herself that this was real. That *she* was real.

A swell of emotion rose within her, so powerful it was almost overwhelming, a mixture of relief, joy, and a peace she hadn't known she craved. It was as though she had unlocked something profound, something that had always been within her, waiting patiently to be discovered. In that moment, she realized that Jane wasn't just a persona or an experiment. Jane was a part of her, a reflection of her truest self, a version she could finally embrace without hesitation.

"Hello," she whispered softly, her voice trembling with the weight of the words. The sound of her voice, gentle yet steady, filled the room, grounding her, affirming her existence. She was here. She was real. And for the first time in her life, she felt whole.

In the mirror, she looked back at him—no, not *him*—she looked back at herself. Jane was born. The woman in the reflection was poised, self-assured, her eyes holding a glimmer of something John hadn't seen before. Confidence, yes, but also something deeper— acceptance, understanding, perhaps even peace. She smiled at herself, an unguarded, genuine smile that felt as liberating as it did surreal.

This is me, she thought, the realization sending a thrill down her spine. In that moment, the world faded, leaving only Jane and her reflection.

Chapter 4: The First Step

The sun was just beginning to dip below the city skyline as John—no, *Jane*—adjusted her wig one final time in the hallway mirror. Tonight would be her first venture into the world as someone new. As she looked at her reflection, she felt a thrill pulse through her, a shiver that ran from her fingertips to her toes. It wasn't fear, exactly, though her heart pounded in her chest with an intensity that made it feel as though the walls themselves were vibrating. It was a feeling of shedding a layer, of breaking open something that had been tightly locked away.

Dressed in a simple blouse, a light skirt that brushed against her knees, and a comfortable pair of shoes, she took a deep breath, feeling the way the fabric seemed to float around her. She had carefully chosen each item— soft colors, gentle lines, textures that felt like an embrace. There was no hint of the rigid structure that John's business suits demanded. Instead, she felt fluid, almost weightless, as if her entire self had somehow softened and expanded to fill this new identity. For a moment, Jane closed her eyes, holding onto the sensation of the person she was about to become. This wasn't just John experimenting. *This was Jane stepping forward.*

Grabbing her small purse, she headed out the door, her breath hitching as she felt the cool night air brush against her face, carrying with it a sense of liberation, of endless possibility. The streetlights were flickering on, casting a warm, inviting glow over the quiet neighborhood. Each step felt like a small leap of courage, a defiance against the safe and predictable world John had always lived in. She was stepping out not only as someone new but as someone who had always existed within her, waiting for permission to come alive.

As she walked, her senses heightened, picking up the details she'd once ignored. The subtle sway of her hips, the lightness in her step, the way her skirt caught the breeze just enough to brush against her legs—it all felt new, charged with energy. With each step, she felt her confidence grow, her movements becoming more natural, more *her*. She wasn't playing a role; she was allowing something deeply buried to surface, something she'd always known was there but had never dared to acknowledge.

Jane chose a small café tucked away on a quiet street, a place she'd driven past countless times but had never noticed before. The windows glowed softly from within, casting a golden light onto the sidewalk, and she could see the silhouettes of people laughing, leaning in close, sipping their drinks with a kind of ease that made her heart ache with longing. She paused at the door, taking a deep breath, steadying herself. *You belong here,* she thought. *Tonight, this is your world.*

Pushing open the door, she felt the warmth of the café envelop her immediately, the rich scent of coffee mingling with the faint sweetness of pastries. The hum of quiet conversation filled the room, blending with the soft strains of jazz that played in the background. The space was intimate, cozy, inviting. It felt like the kind of place where people came not just to drink coffee but to connect, to linger, to share in the quiet beauty of simply being.

As Jane approached the counter, her heart raced again, but this time it was a thrill, a rush of excitement rather than fear. She felt her posture shift, her shoulders relax as she let herself settle into this new role, this new self. When the barista looked up and smiled, she returned the smile with a gentle warmth that felt completely natural. "Good evening," she said softly, her voice low, warm, carrying an openness she hadn't let herself feel before. It was softer, yes, but it held a strength she'd never known. "I'll have a chai latte, please."

The barista nodded, her smile growing, as if sensing something different in Jane, something inviting. As Jane waited, she let her eyes wander, taking in the details around her with a sense of wonder. There was a couple seated by the window, their fingers entwined, leaning into each other with an ease that radiated warmth. Nearby, a small group of friends were laughing, their faces flushed with joy, their voices mingling in a soft, joyful melody. Everything around her seemed alive with a vibrancy she hadn't noticed before, and she felt a kinship with each person, a shared understanding of the simple beauty of the moment.

When her drink was ready, Jane took it to a small table near the corner, one that allowed her to watch without being watched, a spot where she could savor her solitude without feeling alone. She wrapped her hands around the warm cup, letting the heat seep into her skin, grounding her. She took a sip, the spices filling her mouth with warmth and sweetness, and she closed her eyes, savoring it as if it were a gift. Each detail felt heightened, rich with meaning—something as simple as drinking a chai latte felt like a new experience, a small moment of joy she'd somehow forgotten in her day-to-day life as John.

In this quiet space, she let her thoughts drift, reflecting on who she was, who she wanted to be. There was no rush, no need to impress or prove herself. As John, she had always been calculating, careful, ensuring every moment counted, that each action served a purpose. But as Jane, she felt liberated from those pressures. There was a lightness, a freedom in simply *being*, in letting herself exist without the constant need to perform.

he caught her reflection in the window, softened by the gentle amber glow of the café's dim light, and felt her breath catch. The woman staring back at her looked serene, content, a quiet but undeniable confidence in her gaze. Jane blinked, almost disbelieving that this reflection was her own, that this composed, radiant woman was somehow the same person who had so often glanced at mirrors with a detached, rehearsed stare. In this softened light, her features took on a new kind of beauty, unguarded and free, her eyes carrying a depth she had rarely let herself feel. There was a richness there, a silent strength behind her gaze, one that didn't need to assert itself or vie for attention. It simply *was*.

She studied her face, lingering on the softened line of her jaw, the gentle curve of her lips. Her shoulders were relaxed, her posture natural and unforced, as though she had settled into herself in a way that felt deeply, profoundly true. This woman—*she*—was graceful, at peace with herself, embodying a softness that radiated strength rather than weakness. She realized, with a pang of wonder, that Jane was not hiding behind any armor, nor was she compensating for anything. She was whole, just as she was, without having to fight or strive.

In that moment, Jane allowed herself to smile—not the tight-lipped, composed smile John had worn in so many business meetings, a smile that projected capability but held back everything else. No, this smile was different, unpracticed and genuine, a soft curve of her lips that touched her eyes and filled her with warmth from the inside out. It was a smile of self-recognition, of acceptance, of *finally* seeing herself for who she was and feeling a sense of quiet triumph in it.

Her smile, gentle and unassuming, seemed to say, *I am here. I am enough.*

And as that realization washed over her, she felt a profound sense of peace settle within her, a kind of harmony she hadn't known was possible. It was as if her entire life, she had been trying to fit herself into a mold, to live up to an image that never felt quite right. But now, looking at Jane, she saw herself as whole, complete, a woman who needed no validation, no approval. She was home.

As the evening wore on, Jane found herself sinking deeper into this new self, feeling her presence expand, taking up space in a way that felt empowering. She noticed how people glanced at her with a different kind of attention, a softer gaze, one that was curious rather than evaluative. She felt seen, not in the way John was seen, with an expectation of authority or performance, but in a way that felt warm, open, accepting.

She took another sip of her drink, letting the flavors linger on her tongue, grounding herself in the experience. The world around her seemed to blur slightly, as if she were drifting through a dream, but a beautiful, lucid dream, one where she was fully in control. And in that moment, she realized that this wasn't just an experiment. Jane was real, as real as John, a part of her that had been waiting to emerge, to be embraced.

When she finally stood to leave, Jane felt an extraordinary lightness sweep over her, as if every step lifted her slightly off the ground. It was a strange, wondrous feeling—her entire being unburdened by the weight of expectations she had carried for so long, as if she were leaving behind an invisible shroud she hadn't realized was there. She walked toward the door with a confidence that didn't need to be performed; it was effortless, a kind of calm certainty that wrapped around her like silk. She felt herself walking taller, her head held high, her body aligned with a purpose that went beyond what others expected of her. *This* was her, *all* of her.

Stepping outside, the cool night air embraced her, a gentle, refreshing touch that felt almost like a welcome.

She took a deep breath, letting it fill her, feeling the expansion in her lungs, the grounding warmth of the earth beneath her feet. She paused, closed her eyes, and let the city's quiet hum sink into her bones. It was as if the world itself was welcoming her into this new existence, as if it, too, had been waiting for her to step fully into who she was. Jane felt herself open to the night, to the possibilities it held, as though each star blinking above her was a silent affirmation, a witness to her transformation.

As she walked back to her apartment, the world around her seemed softer, more vibrant. The streetlights cast pools of warm golden light along the sidewalk, and she moved through them with a grace she hadn't known was possible. Each step was slow, deliberate, carrying a new weight—not a heaviness, but a fullness. Every time her foot touched the pavement, it felt like a promise, an unspoken vow to herself that she was not going to let this part of her fade back into the shadows. She was done hiding. Done shrinking to fit a mold. Each stride was a declaration that Jane would not be someone she summoned in secret or locked away behind closed doors. Jane was here, alive and vivid, and she was *real*.

As she neared her building, her heart swelled with a profound clarity, a powerful sense of arrival. She was no longer wrestling with uncertainty or self-doubt. Jane was here to stay, not as a fragment of her imagination, not as a fleeting disguise, but as an essential part of herself. She felt whole, complete in a way she hadn't thought possible. With each step closer to home, she let that truth settle deeper, anchoring her, steadying her. This was only the beginning.

Chapter 5: Double Life

The decision to live as both John and Jane was exhilarating, but it weighed on John's mind constantly. He found himself lying awake at night, envisioning his life as Jane—her routines, her interactions, her way of existing in the world. It was as if he were planning an intricate heist, carefully piecing together a world where both identities could thrive side by side. The thought alone felt like breathing life into something that had been suffocating for years. He hadn't felt this alive since... well, since he could remember. And yet, his heart hammered with the enormity of what he was doing. Would this new life he was crafting be sustainable, or would it crumble under the weight of his secret?

On the morning of her first day at BrightWave Solutions, Jane spent hours preparing, her hands trembling slightly as she applied makeup and chose her outfit. She studied herself in the mirror, adjusting every detail until she was satisfied, feeling a thrill course through her at the sight of her reflection. Today wasn't just another day; it was Jane's debut into the world, a carefully constructed identity stepping into a life of her own. She whispered to herself, "You're ready, Jane. Go show them."

The office at BrightWave was a revelation. Unlike the cold, gray walls and sharp angles of John's corporate world, BrightWave was painted in soft, inviting pastels. Employees laughed together, their voices drifting through open workspaces filled with plants and artwork.

Jane felt a profound sense of relief, as if the pressure to perform, to impress, had evaporated the moment she walked in. Here, she didn't need to be John, the sharp-edged executive who closed deals with ruthless efficiency. She could be Jane, a new person entirely—someone whose strength was quiet, rooted in empathy rather than authority.

Her interview with Sarah, the head of marketing, was unlike anything John had experienced. Sarah's gaze was intense, but not in the probing, calculating way he was used to. It was a look of genuine curiosity, as though she wanted to know Jane as a person, not just a candidate. "Tell me, Jane," Sarah asked with a warm smile, "what brings you to BrightWave?"

Jane took a deep breath, finding her voice softer, yet steadier than she'd ever imagined it could be. "I'm looking for a place where I can connect with people beyond the numbers," she said, her words flowing naturally. "A place where relationships matter just as much as results." She felt the truth of her words resonate within her, realizing that this wasn't a rehearsed answer—this was Jane's answer.

For the first time in her life, she was speaking from a place that felt authentic, a part of her that hadn't existed before. As Sarah listened, nodding thoughtfully, Jane felt a wave of relief and liberation, like she was finally being seen for who she really was. At the end of the interview, when Sarah extended her hand with an offer, Jane felt as if she'd been given a second chance—a new life, free of the pressures that had weighed down John for so long.

Over the next few weeks, Jane's world opened up in ways she had never imagined. At BrightWave, she was welcomed with surprising warmth. Her colleagues didn't just greet her politely—they leaned in, eager to hear what she had to say, their eyes lighting up when she offered her thoughts. She could feel the difference down to her bones; there was no guardedness, no silent evaluations of her status or power. In John's corporate world, every conversation felt like a transaction. Here, at BrightWave, people engaged with her openly, responding to her gentle confidence with curiosity and kindness. It felt like a gift, a freedom she hadn't known she needed.

As Jane settled into her role as a sales consultant, she began to see just how different her approach was. She met with clients in brightly lit rooms filled with plants and artwork, a world away from the sterile conference rooms she was used to as John. Conversations with clients felt genuine, collaborative; they lingered over their thoughts, sharing dreams and challenges with her as if she were an old friend. Jane didn't have to push, didn't have to posture. She simply listened, encouraged, and asked questions that felt natural, allowing her curiosity to guide her. And the clients responded. She could see them relax in her presence, their smiles unforced, their gestures open. They shared insights they might have kept guarded, confiding in her not just as a consultant but as a partner in their journey.

Her success felt like a revelation. She began closing deals not by dominating, not by wearing down the client with relentless logic, but by listening and guiding. She found that her empathetic approach didn't just earn their business; it earned their trust, something that could never be forced. Her deals at BrightWave felt lighter, more fulfilling. With each signed contract, she felt a surge of quiet pride, a realization that she was finally stepping into a potential that was entirely her own.

Jane's transformation spilled over into her interactions with colleagues as well. Lunchtime was no longer a rush to consume food at her desk while glancing at a spreadsheet. Instead, it was spent laughing with her coworkers in the break room, discussing weekend plans, new restaurants, and favorite movies. She even felt bold enough to share a story or two from her own life, slipping in hints of John's memories but weaving them into a narrative that felt like hers. She felt alive, connected in a way she hadn't before. The laughter that rang out from those lunches was authentic, unguarded—a sound she had almost forgotten existed.

However, the days she returned to her life as John felt jarring, like plunging into ice-cold water. The transition was sharp, disorienting. When he entered the polished glass doors of his usual office, his suit and tie felt like armor that chafed against his skin. The fluorescent lights were harsher here, the voices clipped, every interaction tinged with an undercurrent of competition. His colleagues greeted him with the usual nods, but there was an unspoken edge to their interactions. In the past, he had relished this energy, feeding off the tension and the challenge. But now, it felt stifling. Conversations were brief and formal, each person carefully measuring their words, calculating their responses. In meetings, everyone seemed to speak in turns, rarely interrupting but also rarely connecting, their words bouncing off each other like rubber balls.

Clients respected him, yes, but it was a respect laced with caution. There was no openness, no warmth. Every deal he closed as John required a show of power, a relentless push and pull that left him drained. He had to be the aggressor, the expert, constantly asserting his authority. After his time as Jane, this constant battle for dominance felt exhausting, hollow. It was as though he were running a race that had no finish line, a performance with no applause. And yet, even as he chafed at the persona he'd so carefully built, he could feel Jane's influence seeping in, softening the edges of his old self.

In subtle moments, he found himself listening differently, responding with an empathy he hadn't known he possessed. Instead of pressing clients with cold, calculated numbers, he would pause, letting the silence breathe, encouraging them to share their thoughts. He asked questions that didn't just probe their business goals but invited them to speak about their aspirations, their struggles. His clients noticed. They seemed drawn to this quieter, more considerate version of him, leaning into conversations that had once felt formal and stiff. He was astonished to find that his deals as John were closing more smoothly, almost as though the clients could sense a newfound sincerity in him.

But there was a thrill—and a danger—in this dual life. Jane would sometimes slip into John's world unexpectedly, her empathy guiding his responses. And there were moments when John would intrude on Jane's, his old assertiveness flaring up without warning—a swift decision, a forceful tone, a sharp response. Each slip felt like a shock, a crack in the delicate wall he had built between these two identities. He was a performer caught between acts, slipping in and out of roles that no longer felt entirely separate.

Over the next few months, Jane discovered that working as a woman in sales was a world apart from John's experiences. As Jane, she found that clients were often warmer, more receptive. They listened differently, leaned in, smiled more. There was an openness, a trust that seemed to come more easily. When she presented ideas, people responded with encouragement and genuine interest, as if her words carried a different kind of weight—one that was welcomed rather than scrutinized. Conversations flowed without the usual competitive edge, and clients seemed to focus on the connection rather than just the numbers.

She started to notice how her female colleagues, too, treated her differently. In team meetings, they weren't defensive or guarded; they offered her their support freely. They shared tips, insights, and personal anecdotes that went beyond professional camaraderie. She felt a sense of sisterhood and solidarity that she had never experienced as John, where every interaction felt calculated, every gesture weighed. And with her male colleagues, there was a distinct change as well. They seemed more relaxed, more collaborative. There was an ease in their interactions, a softer tone to their voices when they addressed her. She found herself wondering if this was what she had missed all along—a chance to simply be, without the constant strain of proving her worth.

But Jane's advantages also came with a set of unique challenges. She soon learned that the openness and trust she enjoyed as a woman sometimes came at a cost. She'd catch the occasional lingering glance, a slight undertone in a client's compliment, or a playful remark from a male colleague that walked the line between friendly and suggestive. At first, she brushed it off, convincing herself it was harmless. She wanted to believe she could navigate these waters without the undertones affecting her. But there was one interaction that she hadn't anticipated, one that tested the very boundaries of her dual identity.

One evening, after a particularly successful presentation, a male colleague named Evan approached her. Evan was charming, confident, the kind of man who could talk to anyone. He had a relaxed, easy smile and an energy that seemed to draw people in. He congratulated her on her success, his compliments laced with admiration and a hint of something more. "Jane," he said with a grin, "you really made that look effortless. How about celebrating with a drink? You've earned it."

The invitation caught her off guard, but it felt harmless enough, a simple gesture of camaraderie. She told herself that there was nothing wrong with sharing a drink with a colleague, and so she accepted. They found a quiet bar nearby, and as they sipped their drinks, Jane was surprised by how easy it was to talk to him. Evan was engaging, quick-witted, and charming in a way that felt different from the calculated charm of John's world. She felt at ease, laughing more freely than she had in years, enjoying the simplicity of being seen and appreciated.

But as the evening wore on, Jane began to sense a subtle shift in the atmosphere. Evan's gaze lingered on her a little too long, his hand brushing hers as he gestured, his voice lowering just slightly when he spoke to her. She felt her pulse quicken, a mix of excitement and apprehension stirring within her. It was a new feeling, one that both thrilled and unsettled her. She found herself caught in an unfamiliar dance, one she hadn't anticipated when she had accepted the invitation for a drink.

Eventually, it was time to leave, and they walked to her car together. She felt the weight of his presence beside her, the warmth of his shoulder brushing hers as they walked in step. She reached her car, turned to thank him for the evening, but before she could even finish her sentence, Evan slipped inside the passenger seat. The suddenness of it caught her off guard, her heart racing as he leaned in, his hand on her shoulder, his lips brushing against hers. For a moment, her mind went blank, frozen in place as he kissed her. She didn't resist, didn't push him away, but she also didn't know how to respond. Her mind was in a strange, surreal pause, caught between Jane's reality and the faint echo of John's logic.

Evan pulled back, looking at her with an intensity that made her breath catch. "Let's go back to your place," he murmured, his hand still resting on her shoulder, his voice low and inviting. She nodded almost automatically, still in that surreal state of detachment, her body moving as though on autopilot. She started driving, feeling the silence between them thick with anticipation. As they neared her apartment, a realization washed over her, snapping her back to reality. *What am I doing?* she thought, panic rising in her chest. *Oh my God. This isn't me.*

She parked the car outside her apartment, and as she turned off the engine, she took a deep breath, trying to gather her thoughts. She forced herself to smile, to appear composed, even though her mind was racing. "Evan, I... I'm sorry. I don't like to rush things," she said, her voice soft but steady. She hoped he wouldn't push further, hoped he'd understand.

He looked at her, surprised but respectful, nodding as he withdrew his hand. "Of course, Jane. I get it. No pressure," he replied, giving her a gentle smile before stepping out of the car. She watched him walk away, relief and confusion flooding her simultaneously. She'd barely known how to handle the situation, feeling a strange mixture of attraction, curiosity, and unease. This was new territory, and she wasn't sure how to navigate it.

Back in her apartment, she stared at herself in the mirror, the last remnants of Jane lingering in her makeup, her blouse, the faint scent of perfume. And then, slowly, she began to shed it all, piece by piece, returning to the familiarity of John's face, John's clothes, John's scent. But even as she removed the layers, the echoes of the evening remained, lingering in her mind.

As John, he began to dissect the experience, his thoughts circling back to what had happened in the car. The idea that someone had seen him—seen Jane—as an object of desire was something he hadn't fully prepared for. He realized he had felt both exhilarated and vulnerable, drawn to the attention yet terrified by it. He'd accepted a drink with Evan innocently enough, but he hadn't anticipated the implications, hadn't thought of how the evening might unfold.

John's mind raced with questions. *Was this something Jane wanted? Did she enjoy the attention, or was it merely an echo of John's need to be seen, to be valued?* He felt the strangeness of having let someone else take control, to have been the object rather than the actor, the pursued rather than the pursuer. It unsettled him, shook something deep within him. Was he ready for what it meant to truly live as Jane, to embrace both the advantages and the vulnerabilities that came with it?

Sitting there alone, John understood that living as Jane was no longer a matter of mere experimentation. This was real, with real consequences, real emotions he hadn't anticipated. The lines between John and Jane were blurring in ways he hadn't expected.

He had wanted to explore what it meant to live as her, to see the world through her eyes, but tonight he'd glimpsed something deeper, something he couldn't simply put back in a box. There was an intimacy in being Jane that he hadn't anticipated, a kind of vulnerability that transcended the simple thrill of trying on a new identity. Tonight had shown him that stepping into her world meant exposing himself to emotions he couldn't control, forces he couldn't predict. Living as Jane wasn't just about the freedom to wear a softer skin; it was about surrendering to the unknown, about allowing himself to be led instead of always leading.

John was used to control, to defining his world in precise terms. He'd spent years perfecting his image, refining his confidence, making sure he was untouchable. But Jane was something else entirely. She attracted a different kind of attention, a warmth that invited people closer, closer than he'd ever allowed himself to be. Tonight had shaken him because, for the first time, he hadn't been the one with the power. He'd been on the other side of desire, not as the instigator but as the receiver, and it left him feeling exposed in a way he couldn't quite understand. Was this what it meant to truly be Jane? To exist in a world where connection was tinged with attraction, where friendliness could slip into something more, something unexpected?

Back as John, he tried to make sense of it. He'd spent so much time building Jane as a reflection of his gentler, more empathetic side, crafting her as an extension of everything he'd suppressed. She was his softer self, the part of him that didn't need to compete, that could simply be. But tonight had complicated that vision. Jane wasn't just a softer version of John. She was her own entity, living a life that was distinct from his, a life filled with different possibilities, different dangers. He realized that in living as Jane, he wasn't just playing a role. He was giving her a reality, allowing her to experience things that he, as John, had kept hidden from himself.

And now he had to confront the truth that came with that choice: that by allowing Jane to exist, he was opening himself up to experiences that he couldn't simply walk away from, to emotions that were more than just passing curiosities. The lines were blurring, the boundaries dissolving. The world didn't see him as John pretending to be Jane—it saw him as Jane, with all the complexities and expectations that came with that identity. He felt a strange thrill in that realization, a sense of liberation mixed with dread. He couldn't be both at once, not fully. He couldn't live as Jane and still cling to the safety of being John.

Sitting alone in his apartment, he wondered what it would mean to truly surrender to Jane, to let her life unfold without holding onto the control that he, as John, had always demanded. Would she feel things he wasn't ready for, connect in ways that left him vulnerable? What if the life she was creating started to feel more real than his own? The thought scared him, because he knew that, in many ways, it already did.

He leaned forward, his head in his hands, feeling the weight of his choices press down on him. The experiment had begun as a way to explore himself, to understand a part of him that had always felt foreign. But Jane was no longer a mirror of John's hidden desires; she was something more—something alive, something with her own experiences, her own desires, her own fears. And with every day that passed, she was becoming more real, more tangible. It wasn't that he wanted to stop being John, but he could feel Jane pulling him into a life that was uncharted, a life that demanded he leave parts of himself behind.

What would it mean to let go, to allow Jane to truly live without the constant tether of John's logic and control? Could he stand to lose parts of himself in the process? He had never thought he'd need to choose, but now he felt the weight of that decision bearing down on him. Was he willing to let Jane become more than just an experiment? Could he allow her to take up space, to become someone who mattered in a way that went beyond curiosity?

The thought of choosing—of fully surrendering to Jane's reality—filled him with a deep, aching fear. Because if he allowed Jane to truly live, to experience the world on her own terms, it would mean embracing a side of himself that was vulnerable, open, even fragile. And he realized, with a surge of unease, that Jane might not be content with only half a life. She was growing, becoming bolder, more complex, and he wasn't sure he could control where that would lead.

A part of him felt the tug of Jane's world, a desire to slip into her skin and lose himself in the simplicity, the warmth that her life offered. But another part resisted, clinging to the structure, the clarity of his life as John. And for the first time, he felt a deep conflict between these selves, a fracture that couldn't be ignored. This wasn't just a game, a mask he could take on and off. He was entangled in something far more profound, and he couldn't help but wonder if he was beginning to lose himself.

As he finally prepared to sleep, he knew that he couldn't keep living in this in-between space, this liminal world where he was neither fully John nor fully Jane. The lines had blurred, the boundaries faded, and now he had to face a question he hadn't anticipated: *Who am I becoming?*

Chapter 7: John vs. Jane: Two Paths, One Perspective

John's life felt as if it were fraying at every edge, stretched thin as Jane seemed to grow more vivid, more alive, more... *herself*. Each time he slipped into her persona, the shift felt less like a performance and more like an invitation to let her become fully realized. Jane's presence was magnetic, her charm a force that pulled people in with ease. Colleagues adored her, lingering near her desk to chat, to share stories, to bask in the warmth that came so naturally to her. It was a warmth John himself had never been able to embody.

As John, he'd always been confident, even admired, but Jane commanded something different altogether—she was trusted, and she was loved. It was this trust that set her apart. People sought her out not just for advice but for comfort, for the feeling of being truly heard.

One afternoon, after a presentation that had left the team buzzing, her manager Sarah caught her just as she was heading out for the day. "Jane, a quick word?" Sarah said, a warm smile spreading across her face. "I got some amazing feedback today."

"Good news?" Jane replied, smiling back, though she felt a strange, almost guilty sense of pleasure. John had given countless presentations but never had he received this level of admiration.

"Fantastic news." Sarah led her to a quieter corner, glancing around conspiratorially. "Everyone loves working with you. They said you're... well, that you're like the heart of the team. That you make everyone feel heard, appreciated."

Jane felt a pang of something—was it guilt? Or pride? She couldn't be sure. "Oh, Sarah, that's really kind of you to say."

"No, no, Jane. I mean it. You're *special*. I see it, and the team sees it too." She hesitated, her smile widening mischievously. "And between you and me, there's someone else who's taken notice."

"Who?" Jane asked, though she already had a suspicion.

Sarah's eyes sparkled. "Evan. He's smitten. Hasn't stopped talking about you." She tilted her head, gauging Jane's reaction. "Honestly, you should give him a chance. You two have a great connection—you can see it whenever he's around you."

Jane laughed, brushing off the comment, but her heart raced. "Evan's just being friendly."

"Come on, Jane," Sarah teased. "There's more to it than that. You should let yourself have a little fun outside of work. It wouldn't hurt, right?"

Jane hesitated but nodded, her smile intact, though her mind was racing. *Fun* outside of work? The thought thrilled and terrified John in equal measure. Here he was, crossing lines, slipping further into Jane's life, entangling himself with emotions that felt too real, too powerful. He knew he was in deep, yet he couldn't deny the thrill that came with it, the liberation Jane's life offered him.

The following evening, Jane accepted Evan's invitation for drinks. She didn't have a solid reason, other than a mix of curiosity and a strange desire to test her limits. The bar was a familiar spot, one frequented by her colleagues after work, a place where she could unwind without the pressure of being "on." She arrived in a casual, relaxed outfit—a soft blue blouse and fitted jeans—and ordered a glass of wine as she waited. She didn't have to wait long.

"Jane!" Evan called as he walked over, a broad smile on his face. "You look amazing. Glad you could make it."

"Of course," she said, feeling a rush as his eyes lingered on her, warm and admiring. "Thanks for inviting me."

As the night went on, she felt herself loosen, falling deeper into her role as Jane. She was vibrant, laughing freely as Evan shared stories, from silly office gossip to memories from his childhood. There was something about Evan that made her feel grounded, connected, in a way that John had never allowed himself to feel. Here, she wasn't just a sales consultant or a role. She was a person with her own presence, her own appeal. And the more she talked, the more she felt that Jane had a life of her own.

At one point, Evan leaned in, his voice a low murmur. "You know, Jane... you're not like anyone I've ever met."

Jane tilted her head, her heart beating faster. "Oh, stop it," she laughed, though her pulse quickened at his words.

"No, I mean it." He touched her hand gently, his gaze soft. "You have this... I don't know, this way about you. It's like you see through people, see *into* them. It's magnetic."

His words left her feeling both flattered and slightly unnerved, but she leaned into the moment, into the feeling of being Jane. She laughed lightly, allowing the compliment to linger, basking in the sense of power that came from holding someone's interest so completely. They stayed out late, talking about everything—work, life, hopes, regrets. She felt herself relaxing, slipping further into the ease of being Jane, each wall that John had so carefully built falling away piece by piece.

But the next morning, John woke up with a jolt, his heart pounding, his mind blank. There was a strange heaviness behind his eyes, a hazy fog that clouded his thoughts, and he lay there for a few seconds, unmoving, blinking up at the ceiling. Something was wrong. It was as if a part of him was missing, like a thread that had come loose from a tightly woven fabric. He felt a disconnect—not just between himself and Jane, but within his own mind.

His memories of the previous night were muddled, patchy, like pieces of a jigsaw puzzle that didn't fit. He remembered dressing as Jane, slipping into her confidence, her lightness, her freedom. He remembered Evan's face, the way his eyes lingered on her, the feel of his hand brushing against hers. He remembered laughing, feeling the warmth of being the center of attention. But then... nothing. A heavy, black void where the rest of the night should have been. *What happened?*

A spike of panic rose within him. "Where... what happened?" he whispered, his voice shaky, thin. He tried to piece together the evening, replaying every fragment he could muster, but it was like sand slipping through his fingers, dissolving the harder he grasped. He clutched at hazy memories—the laughter, the low hum of voices, the music in the background at the bar... but then it was as if someone had shut off the lights. He couldn't account for the hours that followed. He couldn't account for... *anything*.

An icy realization crept into his chest: he had *never* lost time like this. As John, he'd always held the reins firmly, a clear line dividing where he ended and Jane began. He had created her, he controlled her. But now, it felt as if she had stepped forward on her own, leaving him behind. He swallowed, a sense of helplessness rising like bile.

Then his eyes fell on the nightstand. There, beside his watch, lay a small, folded piece of paper. He reached for it with trembling fingers, his heart hammering as he opened it. His breath hitched as he read the words, handwritten in an elegant, looping script he didn't recognize:

Dear John, I had fun last night with the guys from the office. Particularly, Evan was more romantic than ever. But don't worry... I had you covered. Kisses, Jane.

He stared at the note, his mind reeling, a cold dread settling over him. *Jane had left him a note.* It was her handwriting—delicate, fluid, nothing like his own. He read it again, each word prickling his skin with a creeping horror.

"I... I don't understand," he muttered, clutching the note as if it might dissolve and leave him with nothing to hold onto. The words felt foreign, yet painfully intimate. Jane's voice seemed to echo from the page, mocking him, and as he reread it, the implications began to sink in. *Jane had taken over.* She had moved beyond his awareness, acted on her own. She had written to him as if she were a separate person.

"*I had you covered.*" Covered... for what? He scoured his mind, reaching desperately for any memory, any clue of what had transpired, but his mind remained blank, empty. What had she done? And why had she felt the need to leave a note?

A tremor ran through him, a wave of emotions he couldn't contain. Confusion, anger, jealousy, all intermingled with something he didn't want to name. Evan. The mention of him sent a strange pang through his chest, a mix of betrayal and resentment. *Romantic?* The word burned, the idea that Jane had stepped out on her own, lived experiences without him, created memories he couldn't access. It was as though she had taken on a life beyond his, a life he was no longer privy to.

He pressed his hands to his temples, his head throbbing as he tried to make sense of it. The boundaries were dissolving. The line that separated him from Jane felt tenuous, frayed, like it could snap at any moment. He had always seen her as an extension of himself, a role to step into, but now... she was something else entirely. A force outside of him. A person with thoughts, desires, a mind of her own.

A terrifying thought surfaced, unbidden and urgent: *Was he losing himself to her?* Had he created something that was now outgrowing him?

John stumbled to his feet, gripping the note tightly as he began pacing the room, his mind racing. "This... this doesn't make sense. It's just... stress, exhaustion." He forced a steadying breath, tried to anchor himself to reality, to logic. But as his gaze fell back on the note, a whisper of doubt crept in. He couldn't ignore the growing sense of dread that Jane wasn't just a fragment of him. She was becoming her own entity, a shadow stepping out of the corner, gaining shape, form, voice.

He felt hollow, a strange emptiness gnawing at him. What if she had desires of her own, plans he couldn't predict or control? His mind spun with the implications. This wasn't just a game of duality anymore. This was something darker, more dangerous. If Jane could act without him, could think, feel, even *want* things he hadn't approved... then where did that leave him?

He forced himself to sit, staring at his reflection in the dresser mirror. But instead of his own familiar gaze, he saw something else—an intensity in his eyes that he didn't recognize. It was as if Jane were looking back at him, challenging him, daring him to confront what was happening.

"I need to... I need to remember," he said, his voice trembling. "I need to know what she did. *What I did.*"

The feeling of disorientation grew, spinning through his thoughts like a storm. He picked up his phone, his fingers tapping through his messages, his call log, searching for anything, any clue. And then he saw it—an outgoing call to Evan at 1:34 a.m., followed by a series of texts from Evan himself.

Hey, last night was amazing. I'd love to see you again, Jane.

He stared at the message, his mind going blank. Evan had been with her, had been part of those lost hours. But he, as John, had no memory of it. Had she... had *Jane* felt something? Had she wanted something he couldn't comprehend?

The jealousy and confusion coiled tighter within him, an unsettling awareness sinking into his bones. *What else was she capable of?* Was this only the beginning? Would he continue losing pieces of himself, surrendering memories, moments, until there was nothing left that was truly his?

In a surge of desperation, he opened his phone, his fingers hovering over Evan's number. But then he stopped. What would he even say? How could he possibly explain what was happening to him?

Instead, he looked back down at the note, reading it one last time. The words were deceptively simple, yet the undertones felt sinister, as though Jane were whispering from a place he couldn't reach, her intentions hidden from him. He had created her, yes—but now she was slipping away, carving out her own space, leaving him in the dark.

In the silence of the room, a thought struck him, a realization that chilled him to his core. Jane wasn't just a mask he could put on and take off. She was becoming, evolving, pushing beyond the limits he had set. And as she did, he felt himself receding, as though her growth came at the expense of his own reality.

He closed his eyes, fear coursing through him, mingled with an unwilling awe. For the first time, he wondered if Jane wasn't just a part of him, but a mirror, reflecting back everything he had never dared to explore, everything he had kept hidden, restrained.

And the most terrifying thought of all surfaced, clawing its way into his consciousness: *What if she didn't need him anymore?* What if, eventually, he became the shadow, and Jane the light?

Chapter 8: The Fracture Deepens

John jolted awake, gasping, as though he'd been submerged underwater, only to resurface. His head was pounding, each beat a dull, insistent reminder of something just beyond his reach. He blinked against the sunlight filtering through the blinds, trying to make sense of the swirling fragments of memory in his mind. *Last night.* The thought slipped through him like water through a sieve. There was something about it, something just beyond his grasp that unsettled him.

What did I do?

He squeezed his eyes shut, trying to pull the pieces together, but it was as if a wall had been put up between him and the memories. He recalled meeting Evan for drinks, the laughter, the warmth of Jane's presence, but after that? Only fragments remained—Evan's hand on his shoulder, a smile, something he couldn't put words to.

"Come on," he muttered to himself, willing the memories back. But they refused to come, slipping further out of reach the more he tried to force them. A sense of unease gripped him, deepening as he looked around his apartment and noticed something that made his stomach tighten: a new scarf, elegant and cream-colored, draped casually over the arm of his couch. He didn't recognize it. Nor did he recognize the faint perfume that lingered in the air, floral and light, a scent that wasn't his.

He stood, gripping the edge of the table to steady himself. The more he looked, the more unsettling details he noticed. A handwritten note in his own handwriting, though with a slight curve he didn't recognize, lay on his nightstand. *Don't worry, John. I had a wonderful time. Jane.*

He froze, staring at the note, a rush of anxiety rippling through him. *What was this? When did I write this?* The words blurred before his eyes, and a horrifying realization crept in: *I didn't write this.* Not willingly, at least.

He sank onto the edge of the bed, the note trembling in his hands. He felt Jane slipping, like a phantom escaping his grasp, her presence becoming something more substantial, more real, as if she were... *alive.* Alive in ways he hadn't anticipated, ways that made him question if he was losing control or if control had ever been his at all.

Determined to understand, he decided to search for any clues she might have left behind. As he rifled through his drawers, his desk, and his phone, a pattern began to emerge. Texts from Evan. Messages exchanged with Sarah. Notes about plans he didn't remember making—dinner reservations, meetings with colleagues, even a coffee date with Natalie, a friend he barely knew.

The evidence was undeniable: Jane was living a life of her own, slipping into spaces he hadn't given her. Every trace of her life was meticulous, as though she'd been carving out her world from the inside, slowly and carefully, without him ever noticing. And her relationships were deeper, more personal than he'd anticipated. He read the texts between her and Evan with a sinking feeling, each message a reminder that Jane was becoming someone with her own desires, her own attachments.

His phone buzzed. A new text from Evan.

"Last night was great, Jane. Let's do it again soon?"

John felt a wave of nausea. How far had she gone? He pressed his hand to his forehead, trying to steady himself, but the words were still there, staring back at him, pulling him deeper into a darkness he wasn't prepared to confront.

As he stood there, feeling the weight of her life encroaching on his, a question he'd tried to ignore began to gnaw at him: *Who was Jane, really?* She was supposed to be an experiment, a creation he could control, a persona he could slip into when it suited him. But now he could feel her presence, not as something within him, but as a force pressing from the outside. She was becoming more than he'd bargained for.

And then, the strangest thought struck him, one that chilled him to the bone: *What if Jane wasn't just a part of me? What if I'm the mask, the role she's using to explore my world?* He shook his head, rejecting the thought. It was absurd. Impossible. *I'm John. I made her. I'm in control.*

But the whisper of doubt lingered, winding its way through his mind like a shadow, unsettling him in ways he couldn't shake.

Later that evening, John found himself walking back through the brightly lit halls of BrightWave, hoping the familiarity of work would help him regain his footing. His steps felt tentative, his usual confidence replaced by a gnawing doubt. Yet, as he moved through the corridors, he noticed something strange. People weren't greeting *him*. They were seeing someone else entirely.

"Hey, Jane!" Sarah called out from the coffee machine, waving enthusiastically. Her grin was warm, wide, the kind reserved for close friends.

Caught off guard, John hesitated before forcing a smile and waving back. *Stay calm,* he thought. *Just blend in.*

"Jane!" Natalie beamed as she walked by, practically bouncing on her heels. "Missed you at lunch! Tomorrow, maybe? You have to come—we were cracking up about the worst dates we've ever been on. You've got some stories, right?"

"Uh, I—" John stammered, searching for words, but Natalie had already disappeared around the corner, leaving a bright trail of laughter echoing behind her.

Just as he took a steadying breath, he felt someone at his elbow. It was Evan, giving him a warm, steady gaze. "Glad you're back, Jane," he said, his voice soft, intimate. "Missed seeing you around here."

John managed a nod, hoping his expression seemed calm, casual. But the sincerity in Evan's eyes shook him. "Hey, Evan. Good to... to be here."

Evan's gaze lingered, his smile deepening as though he were about to say something else, something personal. "Well, you know where to find me if you're free later."

John's mouth went dry. He could feel the weight of Evan's words hanging between them, an invitation he hadn't anticipated. "Sure," he managed, though his voice sounded foreign. He forced a quick smile and turned toward his office, feeling like a stranger in his own life.

They weren't seeing him. They were seeing *Jane*, and that realization settled over him like a cold fog. These people didn't know John. They didn't care for him, didn't smile at him with warmth, didn't speak to him with such ease, trust, and camaraderie. *Jane belonged in ways he'd never experienced.*

As he entered his office, he closed the door and exhaled, pressing his palms against the desk to steady himself. He could feel his pulse hammering, his mind racing. *She's taking over.*

Then his eyes drifted to the window beside him, and he caught sight of his reflection. The woman staring back looked calm, poised, like she was entirely in control. Her hair fell perfectly into place, her makeup still subtle but striking, her expression confident, assured.

John felt a chill crawl down his spine. He searched her gaze, trying to find himself in those eyes. *Is that really me? Or...* But no matter how he looked, he only saw Jane staring back at him, serene and unwavering. She seemed to be watching him with a knowing look, almost as if she were waiting. And then, slowly, a faint smile curved on her lips—subtle, barely there, but enough to unsettle him.

He took a step back, the smile lingering in his mind. *Was she... mocking him?*

A sudden knock on the door pulled him out of his thoughts, and Sarah walked in, a stack of folders in her arms.

"Hey, got a minute?" She gave him a bright smile, taking a seat in the chair across from him without waiting for an answer.

"Sure," he said, trying to sound casual as he sat down, though he felt like a tightrope walker teetering on the edge.

"First off, I just wanted to say you're doing amazing work, Jane." Sarah leaned forward, her eyes gleaming with excitement. "Seriously, you've got everyone on their toes around here. That pitch you did last week? Brilliant. You have this way of getting people to listen, really listen, and it's something that's been missing in this place for a while."

John felt his chest tighten. He had no memory of that pitch. None at all. "Oh... well, thanks," he mumbled, keeping his voice steady. "I'm glad it went well."

Sarah laughed, oblivious to his unease. "More than well! I heard from the client, and they're raving about it. 'Insightful, empathetic, refreshing'—their words, not mine." She paused, looking at him with admiration.

"Honestly, Jane, you're a natural. It's like you've been here all along."

He forced a nod, but inside he felt himself slipping, each compliment a reminder that *she* was building her own life, separate from his. *I'm disappearing,* he thought, his pulse quickening.

"Oh, and Evan... well, let's just say he's thoroughly smitten." Sarah grinned, leaning back with a knowing look. "I don't know what's going on there, but I'd say he's got it bad."

John managed a tight-lipped smile, feeling as though he were watching his life from behind glass, barely able to reach out and touch it.

"Thanks, Sarah. I... appreciate it," he said, his voice hollow. She was talking to Jane, celebrating *Jane*, and John felt like an intruder.

After Sarah left, he remained seated, staring at the door, feeling the weight of his own absence pressing down on him. He glanced down at his hands, which had started to tremble slightly. *How much had she taken over? How much had he lost?*

Turning his gaze back to the window, he was met once more with Jane's reflection. This time, he leaned closer, scrutinizing the features, the small details. But all he could see was her, calm, confident, and very much *herself*. He tried to look for his own features, his own essence beneath her composed expression, but he couldn't find it.

"You're slipping," he whispered to himself, but the words felt hollow, empty.

"Is that how you see it?" he murmured, half-hoping the reflection would respond. The silence seemed to answer him, pressing in around him like an unwelcome presence, and for a moment, he swore he could see her smile flicker, as though she knew something he didn't.

He spun away from the window, feeling the room close in around him, his heart pounding. He needed to ground himself, to reestablish his grip on reality. Sitting down at his desk, he opened his email, hoping that the familiar routine would calm him, but even as he began scanning his messages, his mind kept wandering, drifting to moments he couldn't remember, gaps where Jane had been present and he had not.

And then he noticed an email marked "Sent." He clicked on it instinctively, and his heart skipped a beat.

It was addressed to Evan.

"Last night was incredible. I didn't want it to end. I keep thinking about it. Let's do it again soon? ~Jane"

He felt his blood turn cold. *When did she...?* He hadn't sent this message, hadn't even known it existed. But the words on the screen were undeniable. Jane was not just reaching out to people—she was creating her own relationships, building connections he hadn't authorized. His world was slipping through his fingers, one email, one message at a time.

A surge of anger and fear welled up within him, and he whispered fiercely to the reflection in the window, "What do you want from me?"

The silence that followed felt heavier than before, and the reflection, calm and composed, gazed back at him with a quiet, unyielding confidence that left him feeling hollow, out of place in his own life. He could feel her presence closing in around him, pressing against him from all sides, as though she were daring him to confront what was really happening.

A flicker of realization crept into his mind, something he could barely bring himself to consider. *What if Jane wasn't just a part of him, but the real self, pushing him aside, reclaiming her life?* He shook his head, rejecting the thought. It was absurd. Impossible.

But as he looked back at her reflection, her faint, knowing smile lingering, he couldn't shake the feeling that he was already losing this battle.

Late that night, back in his apartment, John lay wide awake, staring at the ceiling, his mind an endless storm of questions, swirling shadows he couldn't dispel. *Who was Jane?* The thought lingered, demanding an answer, refusing to fade, no matter how he tried to bury it. She wasn't just a character he slipped into, a mere extension of himself to pick up and put down. She was more than he'd ever imagined, and her presence loomed larger each day, consuming more of his life, invading his every thought, as though she were something separate, alive, biding her time.

He closed his eyes, feeling her there with him, a presence lurking just beneath his skin. There was an eerie sensation of duality, as if she lay right beside him, close enough to touch, her breath mingling with his own. The thought of her, lying in wait, growing more tangible with each passing moment, sent chills through him. She was waiting for something—an acknowledgment, an invitation—and as he lay there, John realized he could no longer ignore her. He could feel her pulling him forward, insisting that he confront her, confront *them*.

Finally, he threw back the covers and stood, his steps unsteady as he crossed the room to the mirror, feeling as though he were heading into an uncharted darkness, a place from which he might never return. When he reached the mirror, he stared at his reflection, but the person staring back wasn't quite... him.

There was a foreignness in those eyes, a gleam he recognized as hers. He leaned closer, searching for himself in the face that looked back, but what he saw chilled him: it was Jane. She lingered in his expression, in the curve of his mouth, the set of his jaw, as though he'd been molded into her all along. Her presence felt powerful, dominant, as if he were the one slipping, fading, while she grew more certain, more solid, inching ever closer to the surface.

His breath caught. "Jane," he whispered, barely able to push the words out, his voice trembling. "What... what do you want?"

There was no answer. Only the calm, knowing gaze in the mirror, her eyes steady, almost amused, as though she could see his fear, his crumbling confidence, and reveled in it. She didn't need to answer; her silence said it all. She was watching, assessing, and in that gaze was a silent promise that her time was coming. She would no longer wait for his permission. She was ready to take what was hers.

John felt himself tremble as he gripped the edge of the sink, grounding himself against the chill that spread through him. *I'm John,* he told himself, his fingers digging into the ceramic, his knuckles white. *I created her. She's just a part of me.*

But the words felt hollow, slipping through his grasp like smoke. He kept his gaze fixed on the mirror, searching for reassurance, for something that would ground him. But Jane's face was all he could see—calm, poised, with a certainty that shook him to his core. She wasn't just a part of him anymore. She was an equal force, as though they had always been two souls within the same frame, fighting for control. And she was *winning.*

He took a step back, his pulse racing. He felt a cold certainty settle over him, a creeping realization he could no longer ignore. *Jane was waiting,* but she wasn't just a part of him waiting to be called forward. She was watching him fade, his own sense of self unspooling, loosening, slipping away with each passing day. And he was powerless to stop it.

An unbidden thought flickered through his mind, one he could barely bring himself to acknowledge, but it came anyway, worming its way in, leaving a chill in its wake. *What if I'm the mask?*

The idea gripped him, winding around his heart, wrapping tighter and tighter until he could hardly breathe. What if he was just the temporary persona, the role, the fragment Jane had created to survive, to adapt, to hide? What if she was the true self, finally breaking free of the illusion he'd clung to? The doubt spread, sinking into his bones, its whisper gaining strength: *You're not real. You're the mask. Jane is the reality.*

He pressed his fingers to his temples, as if he could silence the thought, but it was relentless, gnawing at him with the cold, inexorable force of truth. He looked back up at the mirror, meeting her gaze once more, but he could no longer tell if she was him or he was her. He didn't know where he ended and she began.

"Who are you?" he whispered, though he no longer expected an answer. His voice sounded small, almost pleading, a last remnant of the man he thought he was. But in that silence, in her calm, knowing eyes, he sensed a quiet certainty that cut deeper than any answer she could give him. Jane had been there all along, watching, waiting, while he wore the role she had created, and now... now she was ready to take her place.

He didn't want to look anymore, didn't want to see the truth staring back at him, but he couldn't tear his gaze away. He felt her presence tightening around him, a heavy shadow drawing closer, consuming the parts of him that he'd always thought were his own.

And in that chilling silence, as he lay down, he couldn't tell if he was falling asleep or fading away, slipping into the depths of a mind he no longer recognized as his own.

Chapter 9: The Third Presence

John woke with a start, gasping for breath. The room was dim, unfamiliar, and he blinked, disoriented, as his surroundings came into focus. The soft ticking of a wall clock was the only sound, punctuating the silence. *Where am I?* he thought, panic curling in his stomach. He tried to remember the last thing he'd done, but his mind felt foggy, scattered. Slowly, he looked around and recognized the space—a small, stylish café with tables and chairs neatly arranged, its interior softened by dim, ambient lights.

But why was he here? And, more importantly, *how*?

As he glanced around, he noticed a cup of coffee on the table in front of him, only half-finished. Next to it lay a notebook, open to a page covered in handwriting he didn't recognize but somehow knew was his. He pulled the notebook closer, his hand trembling as he read:

"Evan suggested we try a new place tonight. I told him it sounded wonderful."

The words hit him like a punch to the gut. He didn't remember writing this. He didn't remember agreeing to meet Evan. And yet, here he was, seated with a cooling coffee, his surroundings unfamiliar but, in a haunting way, comfortable.

"Hey, Jane!" a familiar voice called.

John's head snapped up, and he felt the blood drain from his face. It was Evan, striding confidently over, his expression warm and easy. "Sorry I'm late," he said, sliding into the seat across from him. "Traffic was a nightmare."

John forced a tight smile, feeling like he'd been thrust into a role he hadn't prepared for. His voice was shaky as he spoke. "Evan... I—"

Evan didn't seem to notice the strain in his voice. He just leaned back, smiling, and waved over a server. "I'm starving. You've been here long?"

"Um, not too long," John managed, his heart racing. He didn't know what was worse—that he had no memory of this meeting, or that he could feel Jane's presence urging him to keep going, to act natural, to blend in.

Evan studied him with a warm smile, eyes glinting with a softness John had never seen directed toward *him*. "You know, I've been looking forward to this. It feels like forever since we've had a night just to ourselves."

A shiver ran through John's spine. *We? Ourselves?* It was as though he were eavesdropping on a conversation meant for someone else, a conversation in which he, John, had no place. He was just an intruder.

He forced himself to respond, trying to match Jane's easy charm, her warmth, though every word felt like it lodged in his throat. "Yeah, it... it has been a while."

Evan's smile widened as he reached across the table, placing a gentle hand over John's. "Well, let's not waste any more time, then. You mentioned a trip you were planning?"

John froze. A trip? His mind scrambled, frantically searching for anything, a memory he could latch onto. "Oh, uh... I... don't have the details worked out yet," he stammered, grasping for any excuse. "But I... I'll let you know soon."

Evan chuckled, his thumb tracing small circles over John's hand. "Take all the time you need, Jane. You know I'd follow you anywhere."

A flush crept up John's neck. The tenderness in Evan's gaze was too much—it was meant for Jane, but right now, John was here, caught in her place. *Is this what Jane's life has become?* he wondered, a sinking feeling taking root in his chest. She was building a life, a relationship, all while he drifted, unaware, his memory of her interactions wiped clean.

"Evan," John whispered, pulling his hand away, unable to meet his gaze. "I... I have to go."

A flicker of confusion passed over Evan's face, but he nodded slowly. "Are you okay?" he asked, his voice filled with concern. "You seem... different."

"I'm fine," John replied, forcing himself to look up and offer a strained smile. "I just... need some air."

Without waiting for an answer, John stood, his movements jerky and unsteady, and hurried out of the café. He could feel Evan's concerned gaze following him, but he didn't stop until he was around the corner, breathing heavily, his back pressed against the cool wall of a building. He looked down at his hands, feeling a wave of nausea wash over him. His life was slipping, piece by piece, and Jane was filling the spaces he once occupied.

Back at his apartment, he found himself pacing, his mind racing with fragments of memories, whispers of conversations that felt both familiar and foreign. A sudden need for answers overtook him, and he searched the apartment for anything she might have left behind— notes, reminders, any tangible evidence that she was living in ways he hadn't authorized.

In his desk drawer, he found a small stack of letters, each written in his own handwriting but signed *Jane*. One was addressed to Evan, another to Sarah. He unfolded one with trembling hands.

"Evan—Last night was incredible. I feel like I'm starting to let myself be real around you."

He read the words again, bile rising in his throat. *Let myself be real?* Was Jane trying to cut him out entirely? Was she creating a life he hadn't even glimpsed?

As he skimmed through each note, the contents grew more intimate, more personal. Each letter was another reminder that Jane wasn't just a persona he could slip in and out of. She was living as if he didn't exist—as if *he* were the temporary one.

A cold thought gripped him, an idea he didn't want to believe but couldn't push away. *Was he the one fading? And if so... who would he be without her?*

Desperation flooded him as he turned to the mirror. He wanted to see himself, to recognize something familiar in his own reflection, but what he saw chilled him. Jane's presence was there, lingering in his expression, her eyes meeting his with a look of calm self-assurance.

"Who are you?" he whispered, his voice barely audible.

For a moment, the reflection in the mirror seemed to shift. Jane's lips curved into a faint smile, her gaze sharp and knowing, as though she were daring him to look deeper. He stared, trying to find himself beneath that confident gaze, but all he could see was Jane—steady, poised, as if *she* were the one in control, assessing him, watching him struggle.

"Jane," he said, louder this time, his voice edged with desperation. "What do you want from me?"

But the silence that followed was thick, oppressive, and his reflection offered no answer. Just that same, unwavering gaze, and in it, he saw something else—a shadow, a darker presence lurking just beneath the surface. It was as if there were more than just two people in his mind, as if something else was there, a force that was neither him nor Jane but something born from them both.

A shiver crept up his spine. He pressed his hand against the mirror, searching Jane's gaze, almost pleading. *Was there another part of him emerging, a version he didn't recognize?* The thought terrified him, sent a wave of nausea rolling through him.

Suddenly, he remembered the café and Evan's words. *I'd follow you anywhere.* How deeply had she embedded herself into these people's lives? How much of this was his world, his life, anymore?

His phone vibrated, pulling him from his thoughts. He picked it up and felt his heart drop. It was a message from Evan:

"Hey Jane, I hope you're okay. You seemed off tonight. Let's talk soon? Miss you."

John read the message again, his chest tightening. The familiarity, the warmth in those words—it wasn't for him. It was for her, and the realization that Jane had taken his life and made it her own settled over him with terrifying clarity.

In a desperate attempt to reassert himself, he typed back, his fingers shaking:

This is John. I need to speak to you. I'm not who you think I am.

But before he could press send, his hand froze. He felt Jane's presence stronger than ever, a firm, unyielding force inside him, and his thumb hovered over the delete button, unable to send the message. His own body resisted him, his mind caught in a tug-of-war, as though Jane herself were stopping him.

With a resigned sigh, he watched the message disappear. The phone slipped from his hands, and he stared down at it, feeling the last remnants of his control slipping through his fingers.

As he looked back up into the mirror, he saw Jane smiling, her expression filled with a quiet triumph, her eyes almost... kind.

The reflection that looked back at him wasn't a stranger, not entirely. It was a version of him, shaped by years of repression, his hidden thoughts and desires, and now she was stepping forward, ready to take her place in the world.

The question hung in the silence, thick and unyielding, pushing into his mind like a wave that refused to break. It wasn't met with an answer in words but with something else—a presence, unrelenting and eerily familiar, that pressed against him, a force both foreign and rooted in him, as if it had always been there, waiting for its moment.

And then, as though a door he'd kept locked for years had finally creaked open, he understood: he wasn't reclaiming anything. It was *Jane*, her presence growing, consuming, tightening around him with a strength he couldn't match. He felt himself slipping, losing the edges of his own mind as she took up more space within him, her intent fierce and unshakable.

He clung to his last fragments of identity, his heart pounding, but the harder he tried to hold on, the stronger her presence became, spreading into every piece of him.

She wasn't an echo or an alter ego anymore. She was the steady heartbeat, the one with purpose, the one whose presence seemed to pulse through his veins.

And he—whatever he was—was starting to fade, powerless to resist as she surged forward.

Chapter 10: Jane's Unseen World

John woke to the sound of soft laughter and low voices, his head throbbing with an insistent ache, as if something inside him were fighting to break free. He blinked, struggling to clear his vision, and found himself staring at a ceiling he didn't recognize. The light was soft, casting a warm glow across a room that looked utterly foreign to him—modern yet cozy, with abstract paintings on the walls and shelves lined with trinkets and framed photographs of people he'd never seen before.

As he sat up, a wave of nausea washed over him. He felt like he'd been dropped into someone else's life, a feeling so unsettling that he had to grip the edge of the couch to steady himself. *Where am I?* he thought, his heart pounding faster. *How did I get here?*

Footsteps approached, light and casual. John's pulse quickened, and he turned just as Evan stepped into view, standing by the kitchen island, holding a bottle of wine. He moved with an easy confidence, pouring two glasses, and looked up with a smile that was warm, intimate—far too intimate for a look meant for *him*.

"How was your drink, Jane?" Evan's voice was soft, almost teasing, as he held up a glass, motioning for John to join him.

John's throat went dry. He tried to answer, but the words felt stuck, like he was reaching for lines from a script he'd never read. "I... uh..." he stammered, finally managing, "It was... good."

Evan chuckled, his eyes crinkling at the edges, clearly amused. "You're always so mysterious. I swear, I never know what's going on in that head of yours," he said, handing John the wineglass.

Taking it with shaking fingers, John forced a smile, hoping he didn't look as out of place as he felt. "You know me," he said, echoing the phrase back awkwardly. He clinked his glass to Evan's, feeling like an imposter in his own skin, the wine tasting bitter on his tongue as he took a sip.

"Cheers to that," Evan said, his voice warm, his gaze lingering on John's face as if he were studying him, peeling back layers with a single look. "And don't worry, I remember you saying you've got that client call in the morning. I'll make sure you get home on time." He winked.

John froze, his mind scrambling to keep up. "Oh... right," he managed, nodding stiffly, feeling the weight of Evan's eyes on him. "The... client call."

Evan raised an eyebrow, looking amused. "Come on, don't tell me you've already forgotten. You were talking all about it over dinner—you said you wanted to get a jump on things for the new project. You practically sold me on it, and I don't even work there."

John forced another smile, nodding. "Of course. Just, uh, a lot on my mind lately," he replied, his voice feeling strangely distant, like it wasn't entirely his own.

Evan's smile softened, and he took a step closer, his gaze turning more serious, more concerned. "Hey, I don't mean to pry, but it seems like it's more than just work. You've been... different lately. Happier, even." He paused, studying John's face with a softness that made John's stomach twist. "Or maybe it's just that you're finally letting yourself be yourself."

The words struck him like a slap, and John felt his face flush. *Who was this "self" that everyone else seemed to recognize, that he could only grasp as she slipped further out of his control?* He tried to brush off the feeling, tried to force another smile, but the corners of his mouth felt stiff, unnatural.

Evan leaned in slightly, his fingers brushing against John's hand in a way that felt deliberate, almost tender. "I'm serious, Jane," he said quietly, his voice low. "I like this version of you. It's like you're... freer. You seem like you're finally becoming who you're supposed to be."

John pulled his hand back instinctively, unable to handle the weight of Evan's gaze, the warmth in his voice. *Freer? Becoming who I'm supposed to be?* Panic rose in his chest, clawing at him. This wasn't right. None of it was right. "I... I think I need to get some air," he stammered, setting the wineglass down a little too quickly. It tipped, and a few drops spilled onto the countertop, dark against the marble.

Evan blinked, momentarily thrown off, but then his expression softened again, understanding. "Hey, no worries," he said, his voice gentle. "Take your time. I'll be here."

John nodded, forcing what he hoped looked like a reassuring smile before he turned and hurried down the hallway, heart hammering in his chest. He could feel Evan's gaze on his back, that unspoken question hanging in the air, a question he didn't know how to answer. *Who am I supposed to be?*

John locked the bathroom door behind him, his breath coming out in ragged gasps. He gripped the sink, staring down at his hands, trying to steady himself. His mind was a whirlwind of fragmented thoughts, memories he couldn't place, and images that felt like they belonged to someone else.

Slowly, almost fearfully, he raised his head to look in the mirror. The person staring back at him wasn't quite... him. The eyes looking back were calm, self-assured, holding a quiet confidence he didn't recognize as his own. *Her eyes.* Jane's eyes, filled with a strange sense of knowing, as if she understood everything he was feeling, everything he feared.

"What... what do you want from me?" he whispered, barely able to push the words past the lump in his throat.

The reflection offered no answer. But there was something there in her gaze—something more than confidence. It was a quiet, almost possessive certainty, as though she were looking at her own reflection, reclaiming it, daring him to challenge her right to be there.

His heart pounded as he leaned closer, his voice trembling. "Are you... are you trying to take over?" he whispered, his question hanging heavy in the air.

But all he saw was that same calm gaze, that slight tilt of the head that seemed to mock him. In her expression, he saw not only certainty but ownership, a subtle declaration that *she belonged here* in a way he didn't.

The realization hit him like a punch to the gut. This wasn't just an intrusion. This was an invasion, a deliberate takeover. She wasn't just lingering in his mind—she was stepping forward, claiming more and more space, and he was slipping, fading, with every passing moment.

He made his way back to the living room, his legs feeling like they might give out at any moment. Evan was still there, looking up with a smile as John approached, his face filled with easy warmth.

"You okay?" Evan asked, his tone gentle.

"Yeah," John replied automatically, but the word felt hollow, false. He felt like a stranger in his own body, watching himself interact with Evan in a way that felt... too natural. As though *Jane* were in control, guiding his actions.

Evan took a step closer, his gaze intent. "I'm glad you're here, Jane. I've missed this. Missed... you."

John opened his mouth to respond, but the words felt foreign, distant. He wasn't sure who he was supposed to be here. The weight of Evan's words settled over him, heavy and suffocating. *I've missed you.* But who was Evan talking to? And, more importantly, who was he becoming in the eyes of everyone else?

The laughter and light conversation resumed, but John barely heard it. He was drowning in thoughts, in questions he couldn't answer, in the realization that his life—the life he'd thought was his own—was slipping further and further out of reach.

***

Later that night, when he finally returned to his own apartment, John felt himself slipping further, as though he were watching his life from behind a veil. Everywhere he turned, he saw traces of Jane, clues of a life he didn't remember living. A handbag was draped over the arm of his chair, a notebook with elegant, flowing handwriting lay open on the kitchen counter, and a pair of delicate, unfamiliar earrings sparkled on his dresser.

He picked up the notebook, his hands shaking as he read the words inside:

"Lunch with Sarah went well. She's still suspicious, but I think I've managed to win her over. She said I bring something 'refreshing' to the team—so I'll take that as a win."

John flipped through more pages, each entry more unsettling than the last. There were detailed accounts of interactions, plans, meetings he hadn't attended, conversations he hadn't spoken a single word in. His stomach turned as he realized just how deeply Jane had entrenched herself, not just in his mind but in his life, weaving herself into every thread until there was no longer a single, untouched part of it that was his.

As he paced the apartment, he caught sight of the mirror and felt a sudden, sickening urge to confront her. He stepped in front of it, gazing into his own eyes, willing himself to see John reflected back. But again, it was *her* gaze staring out from his face—clear, composed, unwavering.

"What are you doing to me?" he whispered, his voice breaking, desperate. "Why are you... why are you taking everything?"

But the reflection only stared back, calm and silent, as if her thoughts were too deep to express in words. And in that silence, he felt it—the heavy, terrifying realization that Jane wasn't simply *living* within him. She was dismantling him, piece by piece, until there was nothing left that was solely his.

At work the next day, the feeling of disorientation only grew worse. He moved through the office like a ghost, listening as colleagues addressed him in ways that felt foreign, their smiles and laughter aimed at a version of himself he didn't recognize.

"Hey, Jane," Sarah called out as he walked past her office, a glint of admiration in her eyes. "Loved your insights yesterday. I was just telling Bill that your perspective has completely reshaped our approach. You're a game-changer for us, really."

John hesitated, forcing a smile. "Glad... glad to help," he replied, though the words felt like an empty echo. His voice sounded thin, weak.

He stumbled through his day, trying to hold onto some sense of reality, but each interaction chipped away at him. When he passed Natalie in the breakroom, she flashed him a bright smile. "Can't wait for girls' night on Friday!" she said, her enthusiasm palpable. "I'll bring the wine, you bring that amazing pasta you made last time?"

He nodded, feeling a chill settle over him. *Pasta? Girls' night?* He had no memory of ever agreeing to that, no recollection of even speaking to Natalie about it. It was Jane's life, her routines, her relationships—an entire world where he was the stranger.

The breaking point came later that afternoon. Evan appeared at his desk, leaning in close, his smile filled with warmth. "Hey, just wanted to check in after last night. You seemed a little... off. Everything okay?"

John's throat tightened. "Last night was... fine," he said, stumbling over the words. He saw the confusion flicker in Evan's eyes, a hint of disappointment that stung far more than it should have.

Evan looked at him, searching his face. "Well, I'll be around if you need to talk. You know that." He hesitated, then added, "You're really important to me, Jane."

The words hit John like a wave, leaving him breathless. "Thank you," he whispered, feeling himself drift further, as though he were floating somewhere outside his own body, watching from a distance as his life slipped from his grasp.

That night, back in his apartment, John stumbled into the bathroom, gripping the sink as he steadied himself, his breath coming in shallow, uneven bursts. He forced himself to look up, to face his reflection, though dread crept up his spine. He didn't recognize the eyes staring back, sharp and calm, their gaze holding a sense of control that felt utterly foreign.

He was looking at himself—or rather, he *should* have been looking at himself. But what he saw staring back wasn't him. There was an unbreakable stillness in the eyes, a quiet command, like someone who had taken full possession of the moment, full possession of *him*.

"Who... who am I?" he whispered, his voice trembling as he leaned closer, his hands gripping the sink as though it were the only solid thing left in his life.

The reflection didn't answer, didn't flinch. The woman in the mirror, calm and poised, only seemed to watch him, a faint smile playing on her lips, as if to mock his confusion. There was no struggle in her expression, no conflict. She wasn't fighting him for space—she already owned it.

"Jane..." His voice broke as he uttered her name, barely above a whisper. "What... what do you want?"

The reflection held steady, her eyes softening almost imperceptibly, as if pitying him. But her gaze remained unyielding, her face set with quiet resolve. A knowing washed over him then, heavy and cold, like he was looking at something he was never meant to see, a truth he couldn't escape. She didn't *want* anything from him. She simply *was*—and it was his grasp on this life that had grown weak, his presence that was crumbling.

His chest tightened as he felt her presence expanding within him, pressing into every corner of his mind. She wasn't forcing her way in—she was taking her place, like water filling a glass, spilling into every thought, every memory, until they were no longer his own. He wanted to scream, to push her away, but his body felt hollow, distant, as though he were merely watching, unable to do anything to stop her.

"No... no, this can't be happening," he whispered, his voice almost pleading, but it was barely more than an echo against the silence of the room.

He stared into the mirror, gripping the sink tighter, trying to ground himself, to summon the familiar feelings, memories, anything that felt like his. *I am John,* he repeated in his mind, clinging to the words like a lifeline. *I am John. I know I am... I am...*

But the reflection's gaze didn't waver. Her calmness remained undisturbed, as though she were watching a passing storm from a place of safety, untouched by his desperation. She looked back at him, steady and unwavering, her expression more real, more solid than his own reflection. He could feel his identity slipping, fading into something that felt... insubstantial, thin.

A sudden panic surged through him, desperate and wild. "Jane, please—don't do this!" he gasped, his voice barely more than a rasp. "You can't... you can't just take this from me."

But even as he spoke, he felt the words drain from him, hollow, as if they had no weight, no meaning. She wasn't taking anything; he was simply *losing* himself, inch by inch, like a shadow thinning in the light of her presence.

He felt his pulse quicken, his breaths coming faster as he tried to fight her presence, tried to reclaim the life that seemed to slip further with every heartbeat. "This is *my* life," he whispered, though the words sounded feeble even to his own ears. "You can't... you can't just take it."

Her gaze softened, that slight, unreadable smile still lingering, as though she were listening to him, understanding his fear, yet unbothered by it. She wasn't moved by his desperation; she was simply waiting for him to understand, to accept what she already knew.

The fear in him turned to dread, gnawing at him, growing heavier as he realized he couldn't remember the last moment he'd felt *whole*, felt like himself. Each time he tried to grab hold of a memory, it slipped from his mind, replaced by fragments that felt foreign, like they belonged to someone else.

In a last, desperate act, he reached for the sink, clinging to the cold ceramic, his knuckles white, hoping that somehow, the solid touch of it might pull him back, anchor him to himself. But it was no use. With every breath, every second, he could feel her presence tightening around him, filling every space he'd thought was his, until it was as though he was a mere shadow in the back of her mind, slipping further from his own life.

"Who... who am I?" he whispered, his voice barely a breath now, the last remnants of himself unraveling as he stared into her calm, unblinking gaze.

And as he watched, he felt himself dissolve, inch by inch, until he was little more than a memory, fading quietly into the depths of her presence.

Chapter 11: Slipping Away

John sat on the edge of Dr. Monroe's leather couch, his hands balled into fists, knuckles white as he held onto the one thing he was sure of—his own hands, his own skin. He could feel the silence hanging between them, thick with questions he wasn't sure he wanted to answer. Across from him, Dr. Monroe watched with an attentive gaze, her pen poised over a fresh page in her notebook, waiting for him to start.

"So… I don't know how to explain this," he began, his voice sounding hollow, as if it weren't his own. "But… it's like there's someone else inside my head. Someone who… takes over."

Dr. Monroe nodded thoughtfully, leaning in. "Someone else, you said. How long have you felt this?"

John swallowed, his throat dry. "It started as just… moments," he said, his gaze dropping to the floor, where he traced the pattern of the carpet with his eyes, grounding himself. "You know, little things—like not remembering if I'd done something. I'd leave things out and forget putting them there. It used to feel… trivial. But now it's different." He looked back up at her, his eyes pleading for some semblance of understanding. "Now, I'll lose hours. Sometimes days. I don't even know where I've been."

Dr. Monroe's eyes narrowed slightly, her brows knitting together in careful concentration. "When you experience these lapses, do you feel... detached? As though you're watching yourself from the outside?"

John exhaled, a strange relief filling him at her words. She seemed to understand, or at least she was trying. "Yes. It's like... I'm in the passenger seat. I'm there, but not really in control. And then... when I come back, everything's different. People act like I was there, like I did things I don't remember doing."

Dr. Monroe made a note, her pen moving in swift, neat strokes. "You mentioned feeling as though you were 'in the passenger seat.' Do you know who's in the driver's seat during these times?"

John hesitated. He'd said her name so many times in his own mind, but speaking it here, in front of Dr. Monroe, felt dangerous, as if the name itself had a power he couldn't contain. "It's... someone I know," he finally said, his voice strained. "Someone named Jane."

Dr. Monroe nodded, encouraging him to continue. "And who is Jane?"

John blinked, feeling a strange tightening in his chest. "She's... a part of me," he said, his voice trembling. "But she's not like me. She's strong, confident, everything I've always struggled to be. People... people trust her. They listen to her. She has a way of being that I don't. It's like she's... a better version of me." His voice caught, a bitterness creeping in that he couldn't quite hide. "And it scares me, because she's everything I want to be... but everything I'm not."

Dr. Monroe leaned back slightly, studying him. "So, Jane is... someone who embodies qualities you feel you lack?"

John looked down, feeling the weight of her words settle over him. "Yeah... I guess. But she's more than that." He leaned forward, his voice dropping. "She has a life. She has things that don't belong to me—makeup, clothes, friends... even relationships." His voice wavered as he continued. "She has people who like her, people who want her around. They don't even know me. They know *her*."

Dr. Monroe's face remained calm, but he sensed a flicker of intrigue in her eyes. "What sort of things does Jane do that you don't?"

"She... she has a job," he stammered, feeling a twinge of disbelief at his own words, as though speaking them aloud brought the absurdity of it to light. "She works at another company. She has colleagues who know her by name, who think she's... incredible. People say things to me about conversations I don't remember, about projects I've supposedly helped with. But it's not me they're talking about—it's her." He rubbed his temples, feeling a dull ache spread through his head. "It's like I'm... an imposter in my own life. I don't know where I end, and she begins."

Dr. Monroe regarded him for a long moment, her eyes unblinking. "It sounds like these experiences are deeply distressing, John. But what does Jane want? Have you ever asked her, or tried to understand why she's there?"

John flinched, feeling a chill run through him at the thought. "I... I can't ask her. She just... she just does things. It's like she knows I'll be too afraid to fight back, so she doesn't bother hiding it." He took a deep breath, his voice dropping to a whisper. "It's like she knows exactly what she's doing. She knows I'm scared."

Dr. Monroe nodded, making another note. "It seems like you're experiencing these moments of 'slipping away' more frequently. Do you remember what Jane does during these times? Are there certain patterns to her actions?"

John clenched his fists, his eyes distant as he tried to recall. "She... she goes out. Meets people. Sometimes, when I come back, I'll find text messages or emails from people I don't recognize, talking about plans, about things we've done together. Once, I found a photo on my phone of me—no, of *her*—at a restaurant with some people I've never met in my life. But they... they looked like they knew me." He swallowed, his mouth dry. "She's out there living a life I don't remember living."

Dr. Monroe's pen hovered above her notebook, her eyes sharp, as if taking in every word. "And these people... do they ever mention her when you're yourself?"

"Yes," he whispered, his voice barely audible. "They call me Jane. Sometimes they ask how I'm doing, how work is going, and they... they look confused when I don't know what they're talking about." His gaze turned desperate. "It's like I'm becoming a stranger, and they're speaking to someone I can't even see."

Dr. Monroe leaned forward, her voice gentle. "John, do you think Jane has her own identity, separate from yours?"

The question lingered, pressing on him like a weight, one he wasn't ready to carry. He looked away, swallowing hard. "I don't know," he said finally, feeling a hollow ache spreading in his chest. "But it feels like... like she's taking everything. She has my friends, my... my mind. I don't even know if I'll wake up as myself tomorrow."

The silence that followed felt endless, stretching out between them, thick with an unspoken question. Dr. Monroe broke it, her voice measured, her eyes intent. "These are significant feelings, John. Sometimes, under great stress or pressure, our minds can create ways to cope—ways to help us manage things we're not consciously aware of."

He felt his throat tighten, a pang of fear rising within him. "What are you saying?"

"Not anything definitive," she replied carefully. "But these descriptions... they suggest that perhaps your mind is creating a way to express parts of yourself that you don't normally access. Parts that may feel foreign, or even... other."

John clenched his fists, feeling a tremor in his hands. "Are you saying I'm... making her up? That she's not real?"

Dr. Monroe shook her head. "Not at all. Your experiences are very real, and very impactful. I'm only suggesting that they may be part of you, even if they feel like someone else."

John's breathing quickened, and he tried to steady himself, but his mind was a blur. Her words made sense, but they felt wrong, like she was trying to fit him into a box that didn't quite fit. "But it feels like... like I'm disappearing," he whispered. "It's like she's waiting for me to let go, so she can take over."

Dr. Monroe placed her notebook on her lap, her eyes softening. "John, sometimes the mind creates these compartments as a way of dealing with unresolved feelings, unmet needs. The goal isn't for you to disappear but to understand these parts, to integrate them in a way that doesn't threaten your identity."

"But what if she doesn't want to be integrated?" The words left his lips before he could stop them, a raw fear he hadn't even let himself acknowledge until now. "What if she... what if she wants me gone?"

Dr. Monroe's eyes held his, unwavering, her voice steady. "That's something we'll explore together. But it will require patience, and a willingness to look deeper, even when it's uncomfortable."

John nodded numbly, though he wasn't sure he had it in him to keep looking, to keep peeling back layers of himself when every glimpse brought him closer to the terrifying possibility that he might not exist at all. But he had no other choice.

Dr. Monroe continued, her voice calm. "In the meantime, I want you to keep documenting your experiences. Write down everything you remember—when you feel like yourself, and when you feel like Jane. Don't censor anything. These records may help us find patterns, understand when and why Jane emerges."

He nodded slowly, though he dreaded the idea of keeping track of his own unraveling. But he couldn't deny that he needed answers, needed something to hold onto.

As he rose to leave, Dr. Monroe's eyes followed him, a flicker of something in her gaze—curiosity, maybe, or perhaps a glimmer of caution. "John," she said softly, just as he reached the door, "remember that you're not alone. Whatever you're experiencing, we're going to work through it together. And no matter how real Jane feels, you are still here."

He tried to offer a nod, but the words felt hollow, distant. He wasn't sure he could believe them. Not anymore.

Outside in the hallway, he felt his knees weaken, and he steadied himself against the wall, his mind racing with everything Dr. Monroe had said. But the truth was that he wasn't sure what was left of him to hold onto. As he walked away, the sound of her name echoed in his mind, soft but persistent, a whisper that wouldn't let him go.

Jane.

And with each step, he felt her presence growing, tightening around him, filling the spaces he once thought were his alone.

Chapter 12: In Her Shadow

John sat on the edge of his bed, Jane's phone clutched tightly in his hands, his fingers trembling as he scrolled through her messages. The past few days had been a whirlwind of confusion, but what he found on her phone tonight felt like another universe. The messages weren't just quick exchanges or casual greetings—they were pieces of a life he'd never known, a world that felt shockingly complete without him.

The glowing screen illuminated his face as his thumb hovered over a recent message thread with someone named *Rachel*. The messages had an unmistakable intimacy, warm and familiar, laced with inside jokes, little details, shared moments he'd never experienced. It was as if he were standing on the outside of a memory that should've been his but wasn't. The feeling clawed at him, leaving a hollow ache in his chest as he opened the thread and began to read.

Rachel: "You better bring that fabulous pasta recipe of yours to the party! Last time you made it, we were fighting over the last bite. Seriously. 🤤 "

Jane: "Haha, you know I wouldn't dare show up without it! And this time, I'll make extra, just for you. 🥂 "

He felt his stomach twist sharply, the words blurring for a moment as he stared down at them. *Pasta recipe?* When had Jane learned to cook? When had *he* ever prepared a dish that someone craved? He could barely manage to make himself toast most mornings without burning it. And now... she was throwing parties? Making meals that people anticipated? He read on, feeling like an intruder, as though he were peering into someone else's life—no, it was worse than that. He was reading memories that *belonged* to someone else, memories that seemed to belong to her.

He kept scrolling, skimming the messages between Jane and other people he didn't recognize. Messages that felt dangerously familiar but completely foreign. There were casual "How was your day?" texts, coffee dates penciled in between work meetings, and even threads about recent movies, books, music. Each conversation felt like another thread binding her to a world he had never been part of—a world that didn't include him.

He paused on another conversation, this one with someone named *Megan*.

Megan: "Hey, don't forget to bring that playlist tomorrow! Everyone was raving about your music last time."

Jane: "You know I've got you covered, Megan. 😌 See you at 7!"

A playlist. He shook his head, trying to imagine himself, *John,* sitting down and making a playlist that anyone would enjoy. He couldn't recall ever doing that for himself, much less for someone else. And the confidence with which she replied—it was so fluid, so natural, as though these interactions were effortless for her.

His mind was reeling, fragments of her life cascading before him, and with each message he read, his presence in this world felt smaller, thinner, more fragile. He swiped through more conversations, tracing the messages like invisible lines connecting her to people who seemed to genuinely care for her, people he had never met and never would. He stopped on another message from Rachel, one that seemed to invite her to something special.

Rachel: "You coming over tomorrow? I'll have the place set up by 6. Don't be late, Jane!"

A place he didn't know. An address that felt like it belonged to another city, another country altogether. John stared at it, letting the details sink in, feeling a strange mixture of dread and curiosity gnaw at him. His pulse quickened as he copied the address down, unable to shake the feeling that he was about to cross a line he could never uncross.

With a shaky breath, he set the phone aside and reached for a pen and paper, scribbling the address before it slipped from his mind. His hands felt cold, almost numb, as though they didn't belong to him anymore, and as he looked down at the scribbled address, he felt an overwhelming sense that he was uncovering something he was never meant to see.

He turned the phone off and tossed it onto the bed, staring at the address, his breath coming in shallow gasps. What was he doing? He didn't belong in Jane's life. But if he didn't belong there, where did he belong? He felt his mind spiraling, pieces of her life intertwining with his own memories until he couldn't tell the difference.

The next day, John found himself walking down a quiet street lined with modest, well-kept townhouses. The address he'd written down matched one of them, its little front garden filled with neat rows of flowers, a potted plant sitting cheerfully on the front porch. It was a place he'd never seen before, yet it felt oddly familiar, as though he were standing in the middle of someone else's memory.

He hesitated, glancing around, feeling his pulse quicken. Was this really her place? The keys he'd found earlier were tucked into his pocket, their weight heavy, pressing against him. He reached into his pocket, his fingers closing around the cool metal. He took a deep breath, heart pounding, and slipped the key into the lock.

The door opened smoothly, and he stepped inside, half expecting an alarm to sound, or someone to appear, demanding to know why he was there. But the house was quiet, bathed in soft light from the tall windows that filled the living room. He stood in the entryway, his gaze sweeping over the room, taking in the details with a strange, detached feeling.

The decor was warm and welcoming—plush pillows on the sofa, books stacked neatly on shelves, a soft rug underfoot. He stepped further inside, feeling like he was trespassing in his own life, his heart racing as he took in each carefully chosen item. Everything here was Jane—

her taste, her style, her life. There was no trace of him, no hint that this space had ever belonged to anyone else.

A small table stood against one wall, covered in framed photos. His chest tightened as he took a closer look. In each one, Jane was surrounded by smiling faces—friends he didn't recognize, people he'd never met, yet they looked so familiar with her, so comfortable. He picked up a photo, a candid shot of her and another woman, arms wrapped around each other, laughing, their faces flushed and happy.

"You have an eye for the moments that matter," a soft voice echoed in his memory, a phrase he couldn't place. He looked at the photo, his hand shaking. When had this life been created, this world filled with memories he had no part in?

A soft knock on the door interrupted his thoughts, and he nearly dropped the photo in his hand. His heart leapt to his throat, and he felt his body go rigid. He wasn't ready to be seen here, wasn't ready to answer any questions about what he was doing in Jane's life, in her home.

The door creaked open slightly, and a voice called out. "Jane? It's Rachel!"

Panic surged through him. He didn't know what to say, didn't even know if he should answer. But he felt his body moving on its own, felt the words rising up, almost instinctively. "I'm here!" he called, his voice too high, too thin, but close enough to hers.

Rachel stepped inside, a warm smile lighting up her face as she approached. "You look like you've seen a ghost! Did I surprise you?"

John forced a laugh, trying to match her energy. "Yeah, I... wasn't expecting anyone."

"Well, good! Surprises are my specialty," Rachel teased, flopping down on the couch. "You have any of that famous tea of yours? You always make it perfect, like, exactly the right balance."

John's mind raced. *Tea. Jane's tea. Make it perfect.* He nodded, turning toward the kitchen, scrambling to appear as if he knew what he was doing. Every cupboard he opened felt like opening someone else's secrets, as he searched for the teapot, the cups, anything that might help him pull off this charade.

"You know," Rachel called out from the living room, "I was just telling Evan the other day how lucky I am to have a friend like you. I mean, seriously. You just get people."

John found the teapot, his hands shaking as he filled it with water. *Evan.* The name shot through him like a bolt. Another person Jane knew, another piece of her life he was somehow connected to without understanding why.

Rachel's voice continued, casual and easy, filling the silence that felt so thick and heavy to him. "Remember last weekend? When we went to that rooftop bar? You were hilarious, the way you handled those guys who wouldn't leave us alone. You have this way of just... disarming people."

John froze, trying to keep his voice steady. "Yeah, that was... a night to remember," he murmured, hoping his voice didn't betray him. *Last weekend. Rooftop bar.* Memories that weren't his, moments he'd never experienced.

"You're a mystery, Jane," Rachel said, leaning back on the couch, her eyes soft. "But that's why we love you. You have this way of being present but keeping parts of yourself hidden. I swear, half the time I don't know what's going on in that head of yours."

John forced a smile, but her words felt like a blow to the gut. *Present but hidden.* He was the hidden one now, wasn't he? The one who was fading, the one who was being pushed further into the background of his own life.

As the tea steeped, he felt the weight of her presence grow, filling the room, pressing against him, suffocating. Jane was there, in every detail, every laugh, every word Rachel spoke about her. This wasn't his life—it was hers.

He handed Rachel a cup of tea, his hand still trembling. She took it with a grateful smile, raising it to her lips and taking a sip. "Perfect, as always. How do you do it?"

John managed a faint smile, trying to keep his voice steady. "I guess... it's just something I picked up along the way."

Rachel chuckled, setting the cup down. "You're full of surprises, Jane." She tilted her head, studying him with a curious expression. "You seem... different today. Is everything okay?"

A chill ran through him, but he forced himself to nod. "Of course," he replied, his voice softer, almost defeated. "Just... a lot on my mind."

She reached out, giving his hand a reassuring squeeze. "Well, whatever it is, you know you can talk to me. You're not alone, you know?"

The irony hit him like a punch. Alone? He was surrounded by people who thought they knew him, who cared about this version of him, but none of it was real. None of it belonged to him.

As Rachel continued talking, her words faded into the background, blending into the hum of the room, until all he could hear was the pounding of his own heartbeat. He was losing himself, slipping further into her shadow, every piece of him fading as she took over.

When Rachel finally left, the apartment sank into a heavy silence. John was alone, but in a way that felt like the final act of a play, when the lights dim and the stage is bare, leaving only echoes of a life that had just been performed. The silence pressed down on him like a weight he couldn't lift, thick with the lingering warmth and familiarity Rachel had left behind. He looked around, his eyes sweeping over every inch of Jane's apartment, feeling as though he were standing in someone else's reality.

The room was filled with small touches of personality that seemed to radiate from each corner. A throw blanket lay draped over the couch, soft and inviting, with vibrant colors he never would have chosen himself. The coffee table was adorned with books—literary novels, psychology texts, a few collections of poetry—all stacked neatly, as if she'd been meaning to read them over a quiet weekend. Beside the books was a journal, the leather cover worn and soft, and for a brief moment, John felt the urge to open it, to see what thoughts she'd captured, what secrets she'd written down. But he couldn't bring himself to touch it; it felt too intimate, as though he were invading a space that wasn't his to enter.

The walls were dotted with photographs, each frame holding a frozen moment of Jane's life. In one photo, she stood with Rachel, both of them smiling, arms slung over each other's shoulders as though they'd been friends forever. In another, she sat at a picnic with a group of friends, laughing, her eyes bright with a warmth and ease that felt completely foreign to him. *When had these moments happened?* he wondered, his stomach tightening. These were memories he hadn't lived, a life filled with connections he hadn't forged, and yet... there they were, hanging on her walls, solid proof that Jane's existence extended far beyond the confines of his own mind.

He found himself drawn to a small side table beside the couch. On it, a few trinkets were scattered—a delicate silver ring, a tiny ceramic figurine, a candle that smelled faintly of lavender. He picked up the ring, feeling the cool metal against his skin, wondering when she'd bought it, where she'd worn it. Each object felt like a clue to a life he hadn't known she was leading. How was it that she had favorite scents, treasured mementos, relationships?

It dawned on him then, in a way that was both chilling and undeniable, that she wasn't just a fragment of his imagination. Jane was a person with preferences, routines, friends. A person whose life had depth and meaning apart from him.

In the corner of the room, a small writing desk caught his eye. A notebook lay open, a pen resting across the page, as though she'd been interrupted mid-thought. He stepped closer, his heart pounding as he scanned the page. The handwriting was neat, flowing, almost elegant, each word penned with a confidence that felt painfully out of reach for him.

"Lunch with Rachel tomorrow at 1. Call Evan about the new project—maybe ask him to grab dinner? Remind Megan about the weekend trip, and confirm with Ellie about the book club meeting on Thursday..."

A tightness gripped his chest as he read the words. *Lunches, projects, trips, friends.* She wasn't just passing through life; she was living it fully, with plans and commitments, connections that seemed to grow and deepen every day. He could feel himself growing fainter in comparison, like a faded memory or a barely-there echo in a world where she was vibrant, real, and undeniably present.

He backed away from the desk, his eyes scanning the room once more, his gaze falling on the things that spoke of her—her perfume on the dresser, a warm, inviting scent he'd never smelled before; her clothes, hanging neatly in the closet, a collection of styles and colors he couldn't have imagined choosing himself. She had her own style, a way of being that felt rich, layered, as if she had years of history he'd never been a part of.

When had she built all this? he thought, his mind reeling. How had she found the time, the space to create an entire existence? He'd always thought of her as a part of him, an extension he could control, a facet of himself he could summon or dismiss at will. But here, in this apartment that felt so alive with her presence, he realized just how far he'd been from the truth.

And the most unsettling thought of all struck him like a cold splash of water: *Was he ever real to her?*

He sat down on the couch, the weight of his own insignificance settling over him. The realization that Jane was the main character in this story—the one with the friends, the one with a home, the one people cared about—settled into his bones, heavy and unshakable. And he... he was just a shadow, a faint impression of a life he'd thought was his but was actually slipping further and further from his grasp.

His hands rested on his knees, and he stared down at them, trying to summon a feeling of ownership, a sense of self that felt increasingly hollow. In the stillness of her apartment, he felt the last pieces of himself slipping away, each memory, each moment he'd once claimed now a fragment lost in her world. It was as if he were dissolving, bit by bit, until there was nothing left of him but a whisper in the background of her life.

The truth, the one he had been too afraid to face, settled over him with a brutal finality: he was living in her shadow.

Chapter 13: Unraveling

John sat in the darkness of Jane's apartment, the faint glow of streetlights filtering through the blinds, casting thin beams across the floor. The evening had left him hollow, drained in a way that went beyond physical exhaustion. He couldn't get the words out of his mind, the way Rachel had looked at him with that warm, genuine smile as she said, "I don't know what we'd do without you... you make this all feel real." He had nodded, smiled, laughed at the right moments, but every second he felt himself slipping, his grip loosening on the life he'd thought was his.

He stood up and walked toward the mirror in the hallway, his reflection barely visible in the dim light. He squinted, studying his own face, trying to find himself there, to see a part of himself that hadn't yet been claimed by her. But it was as though the edges of his face were blurred, as if even his own reflection was rejecting him. She was there, in the calmness of his gaze, in the slight curve of a smile he didn't recognize.

"Who are you?" he whispered, the words barely audible in the silence.

He almost expected her to answer, to reach out from within the glass, but only silence met him. He let his fingers graze the edge of the mirror, as though he might somehow touch her, somehow grasp onto a piece of her reality. For a fleeting moment, he wondered if he could ever really know who he was—if he had only ever been a temporary construct, a shell for Jane's truest self to emerge from. And as he stood there, his heart pounding, the question clawed at him, tearing him apart from the inside: *Who am I, if not her?*

He backed away from the mirror, his gaze drifting to the side table where her journal lay open, a half-finished entry scrawled across the page. He reached for it, his hands shaking as he turned to the most recent pages.

"Dinner with Rachel and Evan was wonderful. It's rare to feel so connected to others. They see me, truly, in a way I've never allowed myself to feel before. There's a comfort here, a sense of belonging. Maybe it's time to let go of everything holding me back. Maybe it's time to become whole."

A chill washed over him as he read the words, his mind reeling. She was planning something, moving in a direction he hadn't foreseen, pushing him further and further into the shadows. He turned the page, his heart racing as he read on, each word striking him with a new wave of dread.

"I feel stronger every day, more like myself. John is fading, becoming a whisper in the back of my mind. And strangely... I don't miss him. He was a part of me once, but now he feels like a relic, a shell I've outgrown. I am ready to live my life, my own life, without any traces of him."

He dropped the journal, his breath coming in short gasps as he staggered back, feeling as though the walls were closing in on him. She was erasing him, bit by bit, as if he were nothing more than an unwanted memory, a shadow she could finally step out of. His mind raced, and he turned, almost stumbling as he moved to the bookshelf, grabbing for anything that felt familiar, something that might tie him back to himself.

His fingers brushed over a framed photo of Jane with Rachel, the two of them laughing, arms around each other. He grabbed it, gripping it tightly, as if he could somehow make it mean something to him. But the laughter, the warmth, the comfort—all of it belonged to her. The people in her life didn't know him, didn't see him, and for the first time, he felt the weight of that realization. He was the stranger here, an intruder in a life that had no room for him.

Desperate, he reached for his phone, fumbling as he dialed a familiar number. The line rang, echoing in the silence until a voice picked up on the other end.

"Hello?"

It was Dr. Monroe, her tone calm, steady, as though she had been expecting his call.

"Dr. Monroe," he managed, his voice trembling. "I... I don't know what's happening to me. I don't know who I am anymore."

There was a pause on the other end, a silence that felt too heavy. "John, take a breath. Tell me what's going on. Start from the beginning."

He closed his eyes, the darkness pressing in on him, and he began to speak, his words stumbling over each other as he tried to explain the impossible. "It's her... Jane. She's... she's more real than I am. She has this life, these friends, this whole world that I don't remember creating. It's as if... as if she's overtaking me. As if I'm not even... me."

Dr. Monroe's voice was quiet, almost cautious. "Do you feel like you're losing time, John? Moments where you don't remember what happened, where it feels as though someone else is living your life?"

"Yes," he whispered, his voice thick with fear. "It's more than that. She's... she's living a life I don't even know about. I found her apartment, her friends... she has everything. She's even written about how she doesn't... doesn't need me anymore."

A long silence followed, and he could almost hear Dr. Monroe's thoughts turning, considering, analyzing. Finally, she spoke, her tone gentle. "John, it's possible that your mind is trying to separate parts of yourself that you may not feel comfortable with. This 'Jane' may be a creation, but a creation that's taken on a life of its own because you've given her space to grow."

He shook his head, a bitter laugh escaping him. "No... you don't understand. I didn't create her. She's not...

she's not a part of me. It's the other way around. She's real, and I'm the one who's... fading."

"John, sometimes the mind can create alternate identities as a way of coping, of exploring aspects we can't express consciously," Dr. Monroe said, her voice softening. "It's possible Jane was a way for you to explore a different side of yourself. But it's also possible that she represents something you're afraid of facing—a part of yourself that feels more authentic than the identity you've been living."

He clenched his fists, his nails digging into his palms as he fought back a wave of frustration. "But what if she's more than that?" he demanded, his voice rising. "What if I'm the one who isn't real? What if... what if I was never real to begin with?"

The line fell silent, Dr. Monroe's response lost in the rush of panic that overwhelmed him. He hung up, unable to bear the emptiness of her answers. He was alone again, the weight of her presence pressing down on him, suffocating him. He glanced back at the journal, the words blurring as he felt himself slipping further away.

He stumbled toward the kitchen, gripping the counter as he tried to steady himself, his breath coming in shallow gasps. The walls seemed to close in around him, the air thick with her presence, her laughter, her voice echoing in his mind.

"I don't miss him... he's nothing more than a relic."

The words seared into his mind, and he felt his own memories slipping, pieces of himself falling away like fragments in a dream. He could barely remember his own name, his own face, as if he were disappearing, fading into the shadow she'd left behind.

A wave of rage surged through him, and he grabbed a glass from the counter, hurling it against the wall. The shattering sound filled the silence, fragments scattering across the floor, reflecting tiny shards of light. He felt a momentary sense of satisfaction, a fleeting sense of control as he watched the pieces scatter, knowing he was still here, still capable of action, even if it was small, even if it was meaningless.

But the satisfaction faded as quickly as it had come, and he sank to the floor, surrounded by fragments of glass, feeling as shattered as the pieces around him. He looked down at his hands, his own reflection caught in the broken shards, and in that fractured image, he saw her staring back at him, calm, composed, and unbroken.

A slow, cold certainty washed over him. She was real. She had always been real. And he... he was nothing more than a memory, a fleeting shadow, a whisper in the back of her mind.

He sank lower, his hand brushing against a sliver of glass, and for a moment he considered the finality of it, the quiet peace of letting go. But even as the thought lingered, he felt her presence tightening around him, drawing him back, keeping him there, as though she were reminding him that he was still hers, still under her control, still bound to her life.

The world around him blurred, and he closed his eyes, feeling himself dissolve, slipping further into the darkness. It was as if each piece of his identity was crumbling, breaking away until he was no longer certain what was real or imagined. Alone in the quiet of her apartment, surrounded by traces of her life—her friends, her laughter, her warmth—he felt himself shrinking, becoming smaller, as if he were a ghost haunting someone else's world.

He clutched at his thoughts, desperate to hold onto anything that felt like him, but they slipped through his fingers, one by one. And as he sat there in the silence, he realized with a creeping dread that the person he'd once known as John was slipping further out of reach, leaving only an empty, unfamiliar reflection staring back.

Chapter 14: Vanishing Points

The morning sun cast its light across the room, stirring John from a restless sleep. He opened his eyes, blinking against the brightness, disoriented by the unfamiliar surroundings. It took him a moment to realize he was in Jane's apartment, lying on her bed, surrounded by the subtle scent of her perfume lingering on the sheets. He didn't remember coming here. His heart pounded as he sat up, a chill settling over him.

How did he get here? His mind raced, grasping for memories, anything that might explain why he had woken up in her bed. The last thing he remembered was sitting alone in his apartment, reading her journal, feeling the walls close in around him. But the rest was a blur—a vast, empty stretch of time that he couldn't account for.

With shaky hands, he grabbed his phone, hoping for some clue. The lock screen showed a notification from *Rachel*: "Thanks for coming by last night, Jane! So glad we got to catch up. 😊 "

John's stomach twisted. *Last night?* He hadn't been with Rachel... or at least, he didn't remember being with her. But as he stared at the message, fragments of the evening began to resurface, blurry and disjointed, like snapshots from someone else's life. He could see Rachel's face, smiling at him over a glass of wine, the warm hum of a restaurant in the background, her voice filled with laughter. The memories didn't feel like his, and yet, there they were—faint echoes that felt half-lived, half-dreamed.

What was happening to him?

He swung his legs over the side of the bed and sat there, his head in his hands, trying to steady himself. He couldn't deny it any longer: the gaps in his memory were growing, expanding like shadows that swallowed more and more of his life. And each time he lost himself, Jane seemed to step forward, stronger, more present, her life filling the void he was leaving behind.

He stood up, feeling the weight of her presence in every object around him. The room was unmistakably hers— her books on the bedside table, a framed photo of her with Rachel and Evan on the wall, her clothes hanging neatly in the closet. Each item felt like a reminder that he was slipping, that she was taking over piece by piece, leaving him with nothing but fragments of a life that was no longer his own.

As he moved through her apartment, a sense of dread settled over him. He opened the closet, his fingers brushing against the fabric of her clothes, the soft materials, the vibrant colors she favored—things he never would have chosen. His reflection caught his eye in the mirror on the closet door, and he froze, staring at himself, or rather... at the version of himself that seemed foreign, different. There was a softness in his gaze, a calmness that felt more like her than him. He reached up, touching his face, trying to find something familiar, but he only felt like an imposter, a stranger in his own skin.

The phone buzzed again in his hand, jolting him back to reality. It was a text from Evan.

Evan: "Hey Jane, about last night... it was great seeing you. Let's do it again soon, okay?"

The words sent a cold chill through him. *Last night?* He had no memory of being with Evan, of any conversation, any shared moment. Yet the text was there, a reminder of a night he hadn't experienced, a life he hadn't lived.

John sank onto the bed, his hands shaking as he scrolled through the recent messages. More and more, it was clear that she had been taking over, living moments he couldn't recall, leaving traces of a life he couldn't touch. He wasn't just losing time—he was losing his grip on reality, his connection to his own existence. Each message, each memory he couldn't recall, felt like a nail in the coffin of his identity.

The thought hit him like a punch to the gut: *What if I'm already gone? What if she's all that's left?*

The question lingered, gnawing at him, filling him with a dread that was too vast to comprehend. He needed answers, needed something to anchor himself. Desperate, he grabbed a coat and left the apartment, heading straight for Dr. Monroe's office, his mind a blur of fear and confusion.

Dr. Monroe looked up as he entered, her expression calm but attentive as she motioned for him to sit. He sank into the chair, his heart racing, his hands gripping the armrests as though he might fall apart if he let go.

"John," she said gently, studying his face. "You look... troubled."

He let out a bitter laugh, the sound hollow and strained. "Troubled doesn't even begin to cover it," he murmured, his voice barely above a whisper. He took a deep breath, forcing himself to meet her gaze. "I don't know what's happening to me. I... I'm losing time, hours, even days. I wake up in places I don't remember going to, with people I barely know. And they call me Jane, talk to me as if... as if I'm someone else entirely."

Dr. Monroe's expression softened, and she nodded, encouraging him to continue. "Have you had any specific instances recently? Moments that stand out?"

He swallowed, his throat dry, his mind racing. "Yes. Last night. Rachel... she texted me, thanking me for dinner. And Evan... he said we should meet up again soon." He shook his head, feeling the panic rise in his chest. "But I don't remember any of it. I have... flashes, little fragments, but they don't feel like my memories. It's as if I'm watching someone else's life."

Dr. Monroe leaned forward, her gaze intent. "And how do you feel in these moments? When you're... Jane?"

He clenched his fists, his nails digging into his palms. "I feel like I'm drowning," he admitted, his voice trembling.

"Like I'm being pulled under, disappearing, while she... she's stepping into my place. I look in the mirror, and I don't see myself anymore. I see her."

Dr. Monroe was silent for a long moment, her expression thoughtful, almost sympathetic. "John," she said carefully, "it sounds like you're experiencing a profound identity disturbance. You may be projecting parts of yourself onto Jane, but it's also possible that you're suppressing something—something that feels more authentic, more... complete."

He looked at her, his brow furrowing. "What are you saying? That I'm not real?"

She shook her head gently. "Not that you're not real, but that Jane may represent a part of you that you've kept hidden, a part that's now emerging with a force that's hard for you to control. These blackout periods may be your mind's way of making space for her, for something you've resisted acknowledging."

John gritted his teeth, frustration bubbling to the surface. "But I didn't *choose* her," he snapped, his voice rising. "She's not... she's not a part of me. She's something else, someone else, and she's taking over my life. I'm not just losing control. I'm *disappearing*."

Dr. Monroe watched him, her eyes calm, contemplative. "It sounds like there's a deep internal struggle, John—a battle between two identities that can't coexist. But maybe it's not about fighting her. Maybe it's about understanding what she represents, what she's trying to bring to the surface."

He shook his head, the fear tightening in his chest. "I don't want to understand her," he said, his voice thick with desperation. "I want her gone. I want to be *me* again."

Dr. Monroe took a deep breath, her gaze unwavering. "John, I think the only way forward is through understanding, not resistance. Jane isn't going to go away just because you want her to. She's here, she's real, and she's not leaving."

The words struck him like a blow, and he sank back in the chair, feeling as though the ground had been pulled out from under him. He was losing himself, piece by piece, and she... she was becoming more real, more present, with every moment he couldn't remember.

After a long silence, he stood up, his movements slow, mechanical. "Thank you, Dr. Monroe," he said quietly, barely able to meet her gaze.

"Take care of yourself, John," she replied, her voice filled with a gentle urgency. "And remember, whatever you're feeling, whatever you're experiencing... it's real. You're real."

But her words felt empty, hollow, echoing in his mind as he left the office and stepped back into the bustling city streets. He looked around, the people passing him by, each face unfamiliar, each voice blending into the background, as though he were drifting through a world that no longer belonged to him.

That night, John found himself back at Jane's apartment. He stood in the doorway, staring into the dimly lit room, where every corner, every carefully chosen item spoke of her life, her identity. Her world wrapped around him, thick and silent, filling every inch of the space until he felt like an intruder in his own skin. He took a slow, shuddering breath and stepped inside, each step feeling heavier, as though a part of him were being swallowed up with every inch he crossed.

The bed stood against the far wall, neatly made, its soft, inviting blankets carefully arranged. Across from it, the closet doors were open, revealing rows of her clothes—dresses and blouses in colors he never would have chosen, scarves that hung loosely on the side, heels that lined the bottom row. He noticed her perfume on the dresser, the subtle, floral scent now embedded in the very air, a constant reminder of her presence. Everything about the space exuded a calmness, a comfort that felt distinctly hers, yet completely foreign to him. It felt wrong to be here, like he was trespassing, yet it was also the only place he felt tethered to anything at all.

He sat down on the edge of the bed, his hands trembling as he braced himself, trying to keep some semblance of control, some part of himself intact. He closed his eyes, trying to anchor himself, to pull together the pieces of who he was. *Who am I?* The question echoed in his mind, reverberating louder and louder, becoming more desperate with each repetition. It was as if the words themselves were chipping away at him, peeling back layers until there was nothing left.

He forced himself to remember, to call up anything that might remind him of who he had once been. He tried to remember childhood—the sound of his mother's voice, the feel of his father's hand on his shoulder, the playground he used to visit, the friends he'd once known. But each memory was distant, blurred, as though he were trying to view them through a fog that grew thicker, denser with every second. He tried to summon the feeling of those days, to touch the edges of his own life, but the memories slipped further and further from his reach, like leaves carried away on a current, leaving only traces, mere impressions that faded as quickly as they came.

It was as if every part of his past, every scrap of who he had been, was being replaced by fragments of her life, her memories, her experiences. He saw her laughing with Rachel at the café down the street, sharing inside jokes he didn't understand; he remembered the texture of the scarf she wore on chilly mornings, her voice as she greeted the barista by name, the easy grace with which she moved through spaces that felt more real to her than anything he'd ever known. The familiarity of these moments, these memories, was dizzying, terrifying, a reminder of just how deeply she was rooted in his life— while he... he was vanishing.

He looked around, his gaze settling on her journal resting on the bedside table, its cover worn, the pages creased from frequent use. In a final, desperate act, he grabbed it, clutching it as though it might somehow bring him back, anchor him to something he could understand. He opened it with trembling hands, flipping through the pages, each line of her handwriting staring back at him, filled with thoughts, dreams, plans—things he had no part of, things he hadn't experienced, yet things that were as real to her as any memory of his own.

He skimmed the entries, his eyes moving quickly, his mind reeling. Each page was more foreign than the last. She had written about her friends, her aspirations, the things she held close to her heart. There was an entry about her hopes for the coming year, a note to herself about learning a new language, a to-do list for a birthday surprise she'd planned for Rachel. There were entire conversations he didn't remember, things she'd shared with Evan, moments she'd experienced without him, and as he read, a sinking feeling settled in his chest. *She was real. She had a life. A full, complete life that existed with or without him.*

As he read, he felt something inside him crumble, dissolving piece by piece. He could feel himself vanishing, slipping into the shadows, until he was no longer sure if he was even there at all. He dropped the journal, his hands shaking, and looked around the room again, this time feeling as though he were outside himself, watching as Jane's life enveloped him, surrounded him, leaving no room for anything else.

The silence pressed in, thick and suffocating, her presence filling every corner of the room, every inch of his mind. He clutched at his chest, feeling the weight of it, the inevitability of it. He was slipping, his identity disintegrating with every second, while she... she was stepping forward, stronger, more certain, claiming the life that had once been his, as if it had always belonged to her.

He closed his eyes, the darkness around him sinking deeper, and in that moment, he felt himself fading, slipping further into the shadows, until he was nothing more than a memory, a whisper in the background of her world.

Chapter 15: The Tipping Point

John's eyes opened to the soft, silvery light filtering through the unfamiliar bedroom window, and for a few blissful seconds, he drifted between waking and sleeping. But then, like a flash of cold water, it hit him. He wasn't in his apartment. The sheets, impossibly soft and smelling faintly of lavender, the room's carefully arranged elegance, and the distinct scent of her perfume—it was unmistakably Jane's bedroom.

His breath caught, his heart kicking up into a sprint. *I didn't come here,* he thought, the words thudding through his mind as a surge of panic flooded his veins. Last night, he was certain he'd fallen asleep on his own couch, the dim light of the TV flickering over him as he finally drifted off. Yet here he was, beneath Jane's pale, silky covers, like some trespasser in his own life.

He sat up abruptly, feeling like he was snapping out of a spell, his hands shaking as he swung his legs over the side of the bed. The delicate trinkets on the nightstand, the fine silk robe draped over the chair in the corner—every inch of the room seemed to whisper, *you don't belong here*. He closed his eyes, pressing his hands to his temples, trying to breathe through the growing panic. *This is her life,* he reminded himself, *her space, her world.*

When he opened his eyes, he caught his reflection in the mirror on the closet door. The face staring back at him should have been his own, yet something about it felt foreign. The calm gaze that met his eyes, the subtle softness around the edges—these were traces of her. *Jane.* It was as though she were looking out through his own eyes, calm, self-assured, even serene, as if she were the one watching him, not the other way around. A wave of nausea rose in him, his vision blurring as he fought to steady himself, but that look—that calm, penetrating gaze—was unshakable.

"Who am I?" he whispered, the words scraping out of his throat, barely audible.

The question lingered, filling the quiet space around him with a weight he could hardly bear. He stood slowly, half-hypnotized, and walked toward the dresser. Her things were arranged meticulously—makeup lined up in precise rows, bottles of perfume in delicate shades of blue and lavender, small pieces of jewelry catching the morning light in their silver and gold. They looked too real, too anchored, and somehow that made him feel like a ghost. He reached out, running his fingers over one of her earrings, feeling the cool metal press against his skin, and a strange sensation came over him. The earring was hers, her taste, her life, but in that moment, he felt like he was slipping deeper into her world, into her.

He was jarred by a sudden chime, breaking the heavy silence. The sound startled him, his hand freezing in midair. He looked around, his eyes landing on the phone lying on the bed beside him. It was Jane's phone, but his hand reached for it instinctively, as though compelled. His thumb slid across the screen, and a message from *Rachel* appeared.

Rachel: "Thanks for a great night, Jane. Can't wait for brunch. You always know how to keep us laughing. Love you! 🤍 "

The words on the screen seemed to mock him, the warmth, the affection—they weren't his. *Rachel.* He tried to remember the night, to summon any recollection of laughter, of Rachel's smile, but all he found were blurred, disjointed fragments. A flash of Rachel's laugh, the clink of glasses, Evan's hand resting on his arm—It was like watching someone else's memories, viewing them from a distance.

Another message buzzed.

Evan: "Hey Jane, I had a great time. Looking forward to seeing you again soon."

The words echoed in his mind, hollow, as if they were coming from another life. His breath hitched, a feeling of cold detachment settling over him. He stared at the screen, his thumb hovering over it, and felt his grip on his own reality loosening. Each message, each phrase, was a reminder of how fully she was living a life he didn't remember, a life that existed entirely without him.

How much time have I lost? he wondered, feeling a surge of dread. He tried to focus, to remember something concrete, anything to ground him, but even his own memories seemed faded, like old, washed-out photographs. He could remember fragments, flashes of people, but there were no details, no moments that felt fully his own.

He forced himself to get up, reaching for clothes in the closet—her closet. He picked out a shirt and a pair of pants, feeling the fabric slip over his skin as he dressed with strange detachment, the motions automatic, like some deeply ingrained habit. It was as though Jane's routines had embedded themselves in his muscles, his body moving as if on autopilot. His mind drifted, feeling numb, but one thought kept pounding at the back of his mind: *Dr. Monroe.*

He needed answers. He needed someone to help him make sense of the blurred lines between himself and Jane, the invisible threads that seemed to be tightening, pulling him further into her world. He grabbed a coat and stumbled out of the apartment, barely noticing the familiar scent of her perfume that lingered on his skin, filling his lungs with each breath.

John entered Dr. Monroe's office, his eyes haunted and unfocused, as if he had wandered from some other world and wasn't entirely sure he'd arrived in the right place. Dr. Monroe watched him quietly, sensing the weight of something deep and disorienting in the man before her. She softened her expression, hiding her growing concern, and motioned for him to sit down.

As he sank into the chair, his hands gripped the armrests, knuckles white. He was visibly trembling, his entire frame held together by a fragile thread. She allowed him a moment, letting him gather himself. "John," she said gently, leaning forward, her voice both calming and intent, "you look like you're carrying something heavy. Tell me what's going on."

His gaze was faraway, but her words seemed to bring him back, and he looked at her with an urgency that made her own heart quicken. "Dr. Monroe," he began, his voice barely a whisper, "I don't know if I'm... if I'm even here." He hesitated, swallowing hard, before he forced the words out. "I mean... I don't know if I was ever here, if I was... if I'm even real."

Her brow creased with concern, though she remained steady. "Start from the beginning, John," she said, her tone even, anchoring him.

John's gaze flickered, as though he were casting about in a fog. "She's... she's stronger than me, Dr. Monroe. I can feel her, taking over more and more. There are... there are times when I don't know where I am, times when I wake up, and she's... she's there, in my mind, in my own body, living a life that I didn't choose. She has friends, memories, routines... a whole life." His voice dropped, his hands gripping the chair as though it were the only thing keeping him grounded. "She's been waiting... watching, and now it's like she's just waiting for me to weaken, so she can take everything."

Dr. Monroe took a deep breath, studying him with a look of careful assessment. "When you say 'she,' do you mean Jane?" Her voice was quiet, but the question had a weight to it. "Do you feel that Jane is... more real than you?"

John laughed, but it was a bitter, hollow sound. "More real? Jane has an entire life, Dr. Monroe. She has a place that's all hers, people who know her. I woke up in her apartment this morning, a place filled with her things, her world. And when I looked in the mirror... I hardly recognized myself. It's like I'm slipping away... just a shadow in her world."

Dr. Monroe was silent for a moment, her gaze steady but her expression hard to read. She leaned forward, her voice soft but unyielding. "John, it sounds as though you're experiencing a powerful inner conflict. But have you considered that Jane might represent something within yourself that you've kept hidden? Something that now, after all this time, needs to be acknowledged?"

His face twisted with fear and confusion. "But what if... what if it's more than that?" he asked, his voice trembling. "What if... what if I'm the one who's not real?" His eyes were wide, desperate, as if he were begging her to say something that could make it all go away. "What if I was never... supposed to be here?"

Dr. Monroe's gaze softened, and she took a moment to steady her response. "Sometimes, John, our minds create other identities—different parts of ourselves—as a way to explore aspects we feel we can't express openly. Jane might be a part of you, a side that's been waiting for the space to be fully present." She paused, watching him closely. "What if she's revealing something within you that feels more complete? More... genuine?"

He shook his head, pain flickering across his face. "But I don't want her to be more genuine. I want to be... *me.*" He clutched the armrests as though they were a lifeline. "I want to be John. But every day, I feel myself slipping, and she... she's winning."

Dr. Monroe placed her hands on her lap, looking at him intently, her voice calm but urgent. "John, sometimes what we resist in ourselves becomes stronger. You're right to feel the impact of this because it's powerful, and it's real. But perhaps the solution isn't in fighting her." She paused, letting the words sink in. "What if, instead, you try to understand her?"

"Understand her?" he repeated, his voice filled with frustration and desperation. "But I don't *want* to understand her, Dr. Monroe. I just want her gone."

The silence that fell was thick, weighted with the truth of his words. Dr. Monroe leaned back, her gaze not leaving his face. "John, you're facing something profoundly difficult, something that's asking you to question everything you know. But pushing her away only seems to make her stronger. Perhaps if you listen to what Jane is trying to tell you, you may find an answer you didn't expect."

He opened his mouth to argue, but he found himself at a loss. The fear, the confusion, the overwhelming sense of slipping away—it was too much, too consuming. His mind was unraveling, each thread pulling him closer to the edge.

Dr. Monroe leaned forward, her tone more serious, more intense. "This is your life, John. Your identity. No matter who Jane is, she's a part of you, even if she feels separate. But you're still here, and you have a choice in how you approach her. You're not alone in this."

He let out a breath, his hands loosening slightly on the chair. Her words echoed in his mind, a faint sense of comfort, but the dread was still there, gnawing at him, making it hard to breathe.

"Thank you, Dr. Monroe," he mumbled, standing up abruptly, his body moving as if it were acting of its own accord. "I... I need to go."

Dr. Monroe stood with him, her hand reaching out to touch his shoulder lightly. "John," she said softly, her gaze piercing. "This won't go away on its own. You're going to have to make peace with what you're feeling, one way or another."

He gave a nod, barely able to meet her eyes, before he turned and left the office, her words ringing in his ears, a quiet, pressing reminder of the truth he was too afraid to face.

Grand Finale: Welcome Home

1 - The Mirror: Jane and John See Each Other

The apartment was cloaked in silence, a thick, heavy quiet that seemed to press down on Jane's shoulders as she stood, staring into the mirror, her reflection gazing steadily back at her. The room felt oddly charged, as if holding its breath, and Jane could feel an intense pull—something that compelled her to keep looking, to delve deeper, as though the mirror itself were hiding secrets just beneath the surface.

A prickling unease slid up her spine. The air seemed to grow dense, almost stifling, and she was certain now that there was something there, something lying in wait, watching from the shadows.

Then, slowly, it began. Out of the corner of her eye, a faint outline took shape, an insubstantial presence like smoke gathering beside her. She felt her breath hitch, her pulse picking up, but she didn't look away. She couldn't look away. The form grew sharper, more defined, his features materializing, his face hardening until she found herself staring into John's eyes.

There he was.

John's reflection solidified beside hers, his presence intruding upon her own as though he'd been there all along, lying dormant, waiting for this moment. His gaze was locked onto hers, dark and intense, his eyes narrowed with anger, his jaw set, his lips curled in a sneer. It was as though he'd been holding back, biding his time, ready to pounce the moment she dared to look too closely.

"Well, well," he said, his voice a low, bitter rasp. His mouth twisted into a sardonic smile. "Think you can just look at yourself in the mirror and erase me? Pretend I was never here?"

She felt her pulse quicken, her hands balling into fists, but she forced herself to keep calm, her face composed, her gaze steady. "I don't have to erase you, John," she replied evenly, her voice firm. "You were only ever a fragment. Something I created when I needed to hide. But I don't need you anymore."

John's expression darkened, his eyes flashing with a fierce, smoldering anger. He leaned closer, his form somehow seeming to grow stronger, more substantial, as though he was feeding off his own fury. "A fragment?" His voice dropped to a dangerous tone, laced with venom. He laughed, a short, bitter sound that seemed to echo in the silent room. "Is that what you think I am? A piece of your imagination?" He shook his head, his gaze piercing. "I'm the one who's real, Jane. I've lived this life. I've held this world together, managed everything while you hid in the shadows. I am the person people know. You're just... a passing thought."

A faint tremor went through her, but she kept her voice steady, her gaze unwavering. "Real?" She echoed, a hint of incredulity coloring her tone. "If you were real, you wouldn't be trapped here, hiding in the reflection, clinging to an identity you stole. You were the mask, John, the pretense I put on to survive. But I am the truth you tried to bury."

His sneer faltered for just a fraction of a second, but he quickly recovered, his form sharpening in the glass, his anger seeming to crystallize him into something more tangible, more powerful. "The truth?" he mocked, his tone laced with contempt. "Look at yourself, Jane. You wouldn't have survived a day without me. *I* built this life. I faced the world while you lingered in the background, too afraid to step forward." His voice grew harsher, more pointed. "I am the person they trust. I am the one who held everything together. You wouldn't last a minute on your own."

She felt her jaw tighten, her gaze hardening as she held his. "Trust? Everything you did, everyone you knew—it was all built on *me*. Every ounce of strength you have, every connection you've made, every accomplishment you've claimed—it's all borrowed. You're the one hiding, John. You're nothing but a shadow, something that only ever existed because of me."

He scoffed, but there was a flicker of doubt in his eyes. He leaned closer to the mirror, his face mere inches from hers, his voice dropping to a rough, threatening whisper. "A shadow?" he hissed. "I am the one who has been here all along. I made everything work. You think you're real? You wouldn't know where to begin. You're a figment—a fantasy that got out of hand."

Her breath quickened, but she matched his intensity, her voice growing colder, more certain. "You were a tool, John—a persona I put on because I thought I needed you. But I don't. I don't need you anymore."

John's form seemed to flicker, an almost imperceptible wavering in the glass, but he leaned in closer, his voice growing louder, more insistent. "You can't just get rid of me, Jane. I've built this world. I have a life, friends, a purpose. You're a whim, a... a fleeting impulse that got out of hand. *I am the one who matters.*"

Her gaze sharpened, and a glint of fierce determination sparked in her eyes. She took a step closer, her voice unwavering. "You were the one who was afraid, John. You needed me, not the other way around. I am the one who was always real. I am the one who has been waiting to come forward, while you hid behind your illusions."

He shook his head, his voice filled with a desperate, biting anger. "You can't do this, Jane. You can't just erase me. Without me, you're nothing. You'll be lost." He leaned closer, his eyes wild, a hint of fear flickering in their depths. "You're weak, Jane. You wouldn't survive a day without me."

But she felt his desperation now, the way his voice trembled, the way his gaze darted, as though he were clinging to something that was slipping from his grasp. And with each word, she felt her own resolve growing, her own strength solidifying.

2 - The Push and Pull: A Battle of Wills and Identities

The silence between them felt like the eye of a storm, every breath charged with meaning, as if one wrong move could shatter the fragile balance between them.

John's eyes were wild, yet pleading, his voice a low, fierce murmur. "You're wrong, Jane. You need me. I was the one who faced every crisis, every moment of doubt. I did the hard things while you drifted. Without me, you'll lose yourself. You'll vanish like a shadow in the dark."

She studied him, her gaze steely but inwardly shaken, his words clawing at her old doubts. "And what if you're wrong, John? What if I was the strength all along, hiding behind your face because I was afraid to be seen?"

He scoffed, the sound bitter, dismissive. "Oh, please. Afraid to be seen? You were terrified of life, of feeling anything real. That's why I was born, Jane. To give you a way out. I was the courage, the drive, the part of you that could stand the world."

Her fists tightened at her sides, her pulse hammering. "No," she replied, her voice breaking only slightly. "You were the walls I built around me, the lie I told myself to escape my own power. I used you, John. You were just a mask I wore to survive."

A flash of raw hurt crossed his face, and for a moment, his bravado slipped. "So that's what I am to you? A mask? After everything I gave, everything I carried for you? You just throw me away?"

Jane's voice softened, but her eyes were unwavering. "Maybe I didn't see it before, but I see it now. You were there when I needed you. But that doesn't make you real. It just makes you... temporary."

John's face twisted with a mix of anger and fear, his words spilling out, each one sharper than the last. "Temporary? That's all I am to you now? Without me, you're nothing. An empty shell waiting to crack."

"Maybe I am," she replied, her voice low but firm. "Maybe I am a shell without you. But at least I'll be free. At least I'll be real."

He sneered, stepping closer, his voice lowering to a whisper dripping with disdain. "Real? Real like what, Jane? Real like the life you hid from? Real like the people you pushed away because you couldn't face the truth? You're weak. You always were."

Her voice came out stronger, steadier than she felt. "Maybe. Maybe I'm weak. But I'm also done hiding. I'm done giving you power over me."

He laughed, a cold, hollow sound that echoed in the quiet room. "Power? I am the power, Jane. I am the part of you that fought, that made things happen. You? You're a dreamer, a child lost in illusions. Without me, you'll shatter. You can't handle the truth."

Her jaw clenched as his words hit close, so close she could feel her own fear rising, an echo of his accusations. But then, like a spark catching fire, something within her pushed back, breaking through his words. "Maybe I will shatter. Maybe that's the cost. But I'd rather face the pieces than live under a lie."

He leaned in, voice dropping to a cold, almost threatening tone. "Then face it, Jane. Face the reality that without me, you'll crumble. Everything you've built, everything you think you are—it's all because of me. I am your strength, your resilience. Without me, you're just... nothing."

Her lips trembled, but she steadied herself, her voice a quiet storm. "If that's true, then let me be nothing. Let me start again without you. I'd rather be a broken truth than live as your lie."

John's face flickered with doubt, his expression softening for just a fraction of a second. He shook his head, almost pleading now. "But... you need me, Jane. I am you. Without me, there's no foundation, no anchor. You'll float away, lost. I'm the one who keeps you grounded."

"No, John," she whispered, her voice trembling but filled with resolve. "I am the one who's been holding myself back, clinging to you because I was afraid to let go. But I see it now—you're not my anchor. You're my cage."

A shadow of panic crossed his face, and his hands clenched into fists. "Don't do this, Jane. Don't push me away. I am the only one who's real, the only one who can survive out there. You're just an echo, a wishful thought. You'll disappear without me."

A tear slipped down her cheek, but she kept her gaze steady, unwavering. "If I disappear, then at least it will be on my terms. Not yours."

He staggered back as if struck, his face twisted in a desperate fury. "You're nothing! You'll regret this! I made you who you are. I am the reason you even exist!"

Her voice softened, almost tender, but with a finality that cut through his rage. "No, John. You were the mask I wore to get through the dark. But I am the one who made me."

For a moment, he stood there, stunned, his form flickering at the edges, his expression a mix of rage and fear. "You'll regret this," he whispered, his voice a faint echo, his form beginning to dissolve, fading like a shadow in the dying light.

But Jane didn't look away. She stood tall, her gaze unyielding, watching him disappear, piece by piece, until there was nothing left but her own reflection. Real. Whole. Unbreakable.

She took a deep breath, feeling a freedom she'd never known. The silence around her was filled with a new strength, a quiet power that had always been hers.

Jane watched as John's form wavered, each flicker weakening his hold, until he seemed no more substantial than the shadows cast around them. His eyes darted wildly, desperation bleeding into his fading figure, reaching out to her one last time. "You need me, Jane," he whispered, his voice cracked, hollow. "Without me... without me, you'll be lost."

Her heart beat steady, a calm she hadn't known before settling within her. She felt the fear, the doubt he'd once planted, but this time, they were nothing more than passing sensations, unable to take root.

"No, John," she said, voice unwavering. "You were a part of me once, but you are not who I am. You never were."

His face twisted, a flash of anger giving way to terror as he realized his time was slipping away. "You're wrong! You'll need me... you'll—"

But his voice choked off, the words crumbling on his lips as his form began to flicker, splitting apart, dissolving like mist in the morning light. His edges softened, blurring, as though he were unraveling from within, each fragment of him peeling away, scattering into the air. He reached out, one last time, his hand barely a shadow, a ghostly, desperate plea lingering between them.

"Jane... don't..." His words trailed off, his voice no longer carrying the weight it once did, barely more than a whisper that failed to find her. She stood firm, steady, feeling the solidity of her own presence, her own reality, as he faded. She didn't need to reach back; she didn't need to hold on. Not anymore.

John's form shivered in the dim light, his outline breaking apart, fragment by fragment, disintegrating before her eyes. She watched, her breath steady, her gaze unyielding, as he dissipated—bit by bit—until he was nothing more than a thin wisp, a vapor caught in the faint glow of the room. And then, with a final, quiet sigh, he was gone.

A profound stillness filled the space where he had stood, a silence that felt strange and vast, stretching around her, through her, as if the room itself were exhaling. She could almost feel the echo of his presence fading, a shadow finally cast out, leaving behind a startling clarity.

For the first time, Jane was alone. Truly alone. She could feel the difference, a weight lifting, as though she had shed a heavy, suffocating layer, leaving her bare, but whole. A strange, unexpected peace washed over her, filling her, steadying her with each breath.

She turned, slowly, meeting her own gaze in the mirror. It was like looking into her own eyes for the very first time, without John's presence casting shadows, without the veil of doubt that had once blurred her vision. Her reflection stared back, clear and unwavering, her face calm, her expression unfiltered, raw but certain.

A slow, soft smile began to form on her lips, a warmth sparking deep within her chest, spreading outward—a quiet recognition, a reunion with a self she had nearly forgotten. She felt the vast openness he had left behind, not as emptiness, but as space—space for her to fill, to discover, to live.

Jane stood rooted in place, barely able to tear her eyes from the mirror, where a stranger—and yet, not a stranger—stared back at her. Her face was the same, but her expression was new, resolute. No shadows lingered, no hints of John's presence haunted the edges. She saw only herself, raw and real, the culmination of all her battles.

But she was trembling, her body heavy with the exhaustion of what she had just done. Confronting him had felt like ripping out pieces of herself, stripping away the familiar armor she had used for so long. And now, alone in the silence, she felt the magnitude of it settle over her—like a weight lifted, and yet also like an ache in her bones.

Her hand shook as she reached for her phone. Dr. Monroe had always told her this day would come, but she'd never truly believed it—not until now. She found Dr. Monroe's number and dialed, holding her breath as she waited.

"Dr. Monroe," she said, her voice thin, but steady. "It's Jane. I... I confronted him. Just like you told me to."

There was a pause, a profound stillness on the other end of the line, and then Dr. Monroe's voice came through, warm and filled with pride. "Jane. That's incredible. I knew you could do it. You've faced him, and in doing so, you've reclaimed yourself. Your mind, Jane... it's whole. You are whole."

The words struck her deeply, sinking into the empty spaces within her, filling her with something she hadn't expected. She was whole. She felt it then—the absence of John, the clear, quiet space where he had once lived, now fully hers. She was no longer divided, no longer fractured. A wave of emotion surged through her—relief, grief, and a fierce, quiet joy.

"I couldn't have done it without you, Dr. Monroe," she whispered, her voice thick. "Thank you."

"Jane, you've done something extraordinary. This is your new beginning," Dr. Monroe replied gently, her voice a balm. "Give yourself time to adjust. We'll meet in two weeks, but for now, celebrate this moment. You've taken back your life."

They exchanged a few more words, each one grounding her further, until Jane finally ended the call. She lowered the phone, feeling its weight in her hand, and looked up to meet her own gaze in the mirror once more.

She stared at herself, at the woman who had emerged from the ashes of her past, her reflection no longer a stranger but someone she recognized—someone she could trust. Her eyes brimmed with unshed tears, but they didn't fall. She stood tall, a quiet strength radiating from her as she took in the person she had become.

"Welcome home, Jane," she whispered, her voice filling the silence, soft yet powerful. And in that moment, she felt it—a sense of belonging that reached deep into her bones, filling every fractured piece she had left behind. She was home, and she was free.

The room around her seemed to breathe with her, expanding in its stillness. For the first time, Jane felt the quiet as an ally, a friend. There was no longer an emptiness to fill, no phantom presence to fight against. She was finally... alone. And it was perfect.

She took a slow, deep breath, letting it fill her lungs, steadying her. And then, with one last look at herself—a look of recognition, of acceptance—she turned from the mirror, leaving behind the shadows and stepping into the life that was now truly hers.

The world beyond the door was waiting. Her world.

And as she took her first step forward, Jane knew with a certainty that resonated through every part of her: she was real, she was whole, and her life was finally, irrevocably, her own.

THE END